I REFUSE TO BE DECEIVED

- Discover how to identify the deceived and the deceiver.
- 100 signs that you are probably under self-deception.
- Living a life of victory over deception.

FATAI KASALI

I Refuse to be Deceived © 2018 Fatai Kasali

The author has asserted his right to be identified as the author of this work in accordance with the Copyright, Designs and Patents Act 1988.

All rights reserved. No part of this publication may be reproduced, stored in a retrieval system, or transmitted, in any form or by any means, electronic, mechanical, photocopying, recording or otherwise without the prior permission of the author.

All Scripture quotations, unless otherwise indicated, are taken from the Holy Bible, King James Version, Cambridge University Press, Oxford University Press, Harper Collins and the Queen's Printers.

Published in the United Kingdom by Glory Publishing

ISBN: 978-1-9996849-3-8

ACKNOWLEDGEMENTS

To God be the glory for the grace to write this book. I give God all the praise and adoration for giving me the inspiration through His Spirit. This has made possible the writing of this book.

My wife, Felicia Ebunlomo, gave me priceless support during the writing of this book. My two sons, Daniel and David, have been very supportive.

To all those who have contributed one way or the other to the beauty of this work, thank you very much. May God Almighty bless you all.

INTRODUCTION

Deception could be described as the act of being seduced into taking a certain course of action. The person involved is seduced into doing something because the person is unaware of being deceived.

In the world that we live in, the devil employs a variety of strategies to trick people into doing things they would not naturally do. One of the most tragic results is that many people today, after they realise their folly, sadly choose to commit suicide. In other circumstances, people hate each other because they have been deceived about something the other person has done or said. Many marriages have collapsed because the couple were unknowingly fighting over something that was not real. Many people have destroyed their careers because they acted under deception.

The master deceiver is the devil. He has been dealing with humanity for thousands of years and therefore, he understands human vulnerability. He is using his experience to cheat and manipulate people into destructive acts which he cleverly coats with shining packages to attract them into his traps.

This book explores different avenues through which people can be deceived. You will learn from this book how you can be deceived. You are deceived because you are not aware of the devil's tricks. It is very unlikely that you would fall for them if you knew what he was doing. There are seductive spirits that move around in our world to work on the emotions and minds of people to lure them into wrong acts they would not have done naturally. This book explores how the deceiver speaks to lead his victims into deception. In this book you will learn how to identify the voice of the deceiver and how to avoid falling into his traps.

This book also reveals how your old habits can be used by the devil to manipulate you into following wrong life principles. Many people never ask themselves why they think and act the way they do. Personal life beliefs and principles silently control and influence you. You will think and act according to your beliefs about life. Even Christians have wrong beliefs that form our life philosophy and subtly control the way we see life. You will discover through this book that there is a part of you that refuses to yield to the sanctifying work of the Holy Spirit, which the devil cleverly works upon to help you develop ideologies about life. It is possible to be an unloving Christian without knowing it. There are Christians who quote the Bible to justify their error. It is all about deception from the pit of hell.

This book will also educate you about self-deception. I list about 100 signs of self-deception that will help you become aware of when you are deceiving yourself. This collection of signs will enable you to understand how a person under self-deception thinks and acts. If you can study them, they will make you sensitive to the journey to self-deception, so that you will know if you are about to embark upon it.

Finally, the book closes with two major solutions to deception. Testing the spirit and walking in the spirit are the two major ideas I put forward to enable you to rule over deception.

I pray that the Spirit of God will abide with you and continually shed the light of God inside your spirit, in Jesus' precious name.

CONTENTS

1. Understanding deception 9
2. The deceived and the deceiver 21
3. Deception of a belief 59
4. Doctrines of deception 67
5. Self-deception 77
6. Testing the spirits 85
7. Walking in the Spirit 10

1

UNDERSTANDING DECEPTION

Now the Spirit speaketh expressly, that in the latter times some shall depart from the faith, giving heed to seducing spirits, and doctrines of devils...
1 Timothy 4:1

One of the signs of the end times is deception. People are going to face a series of deceptions.

What is deception?

Deception could be described as an act of seduction into performing a particular act. A person is seduced into behaving in a certain way because the person is unaware of the deception. A person under deception does not know that he is under deception – that's what makes it a deception. This happens because the deceiver exploits the vulnerability of his victim. Deception comes with beliefs that are not true or not totally true. Deception could be a corrupted truth.

The power operating behind deception is called the spirit of deception. This spirit, as with all demonic spirits, comes from hell and can attack a person through different avenues. The spirit of deception could minister deception directly into the heart of its victim to deceive him or operate through another human vessel. When a person is under the direct attack of the spirit of deception, he walks in self-deception. However, it is important to state that the spirit of deception is able to make a person deceive himself by taking advantage of the weaknesses of the person.

In the world we live in, this demon of deception is busy influencing society negatively to create a series of avenues that he can use to deceive people and lure them into errors. For example, there are many generally accepted ideologies people hold onto today that come from the pit of hell. There are many policies governments of the world are developing that have come from the pit of hell. Most of these policies create opportunities for the demon of deception to deceive people and lure them down wrong paths.

Many people have been tricked into embarking on a journey that will lead to their destruction. The cost of deception can be very high. It has destroyed people's marriages, destinies, careers, jobs, businesses, health, ministries, etc. A lot of resources have been wasted because somebody acted under deception. Some people have taken their own life because they hated themselves for falling into deception. Many people have been lured into situations that eventually brought them into a demonic covenant—all due to deception.

Unfortunately, the majority of people who fall into deception don't realise it until they face the consequences. You did not know you were under deception because you were under deception. It is very unlikely that you would continue down the path of a deception if you knew from the outset that you were being deceived. Therefore, your claim that you know what you are doing does not necessarily mean that you do know what you are doing, unless time proves it to be true.

Those who are deceived always claim to know what they are doing until time proves them wrong. Many people say they know what they are doing when they embark on certain business ventures, until they later discover that they have been duped out of a lot of money.

There are many people who claim that God has spoken to them to marry a particular person, and they disregard every sign that comes their way to wake them up from slumber until it is too late. When time starts proving their past decision wrong, the same people will start confessing that they have acted under deception. The demon of deception has triumphed over their plans.

Operations of the spirit of deception

Ye are of your father the devil, and the lusts of your father ye will do. He was a murderer from the beginning, and abode not in the truth, because there is no truth in him. When he speaketh a lie, he speaketh of his own: for he is a liar, and the father of it. John 8:44

This verse shows that Satan is the original deceiver who uses a diverse range of schemes to deceive people. He leads them into actions they probably would not have embarked on if they had been left to make their own decisions.

When carrying out his disastrous activities, Satan may deceive a person by using many avenues.

Now the Spirit speaketh expressly, that in the latter times some shall depart from the faith, giving heed to seducing spirits, and doctrines of devils. 1 Timothy 4:1

The above verse and others in the Bible indicate that Satan uses these lines of attack:

1. Direct communication

Satan can directly speak lies into the human's heart to lure us into error.

This means that not every thought that comes into your heart is from yourself or from God. Some thoughts are directly from Satan. Be aware and be alert.

2. Demonic doctrines

Satan uses teachings to deceive people into certain actions or beliefs that are destructive to themselves and others. Such doctrines can sound reasonable and acceptable, but all Satan's doctrines are from hell and so oppose the teaching of the Bible. Such doctrines often promise freedom but cunningly lure people into slavery to sin.

But there were false prophets also among the people, even as there shall be false teachers among you, who privily shall bring in damnable heresies, even denying the Lord that bought them, and bring upon themselves swift destruction. 2 Peter 2:1

False teachings are heresies designed to contradict or undermine the teaching of the Bible in order to lead people away from the true faith or right behaviour.

3. Tradition

Thus have ye made the commandment of God of none effect by your tradition. Matthew 15:6b

Traditions may take the form of a general belief or practice among a certain family, tribe, group, culture, nation or church denomination. Not all traditions are bad, of course, but if a tradition contradicts God's Word then it is cleverly designed from the pit of hell to keep people in the bondage of deception.

For example, it could be a tradition that people from certain tribes should not marry people from other tribes. So, if the plan of God for somebody from that tribe contradicts the tradition, then holding to the tradition will not honour the plan of God for that person's life. If someone from the tribe puts tradition before God's will for them, then, they are being deceived and cheated out of God's best for their life. As a Christian who does not want to live under deception, you will need to stand against any tradition that controls and dictates your life and prevents you obeying God's Word.

4. Human philosophy

Wherefore if ye be dead with Christ from the rudiments of the world, why, as though living in the world, are ye subject to ordinances, (touch not; taste not; handle not; which all are to perish with the using;) after the commandments and doctrines of men? Which things

have indeed a shew of wisdom in will worship, and humility, and neglecting of the body; not in any honour to the satisfying of the flesh. Colossians 2:21-23

Human philosophies usually contradict the Word of God because most philosophy is an attempt to understand the world without the light of God's Word. Thank the Lord there are Christian philosophers these days, who follow the wisdom of God in formulating their philosophy to counter atheism, etc. And there is nothing wrong in having personal beliefs or insight, but they must not contradict the written Word. Therefore, if you follow philosophies or have your own beliefs about life, it is wise to regularly submit them to the searchlight of God's Word, to ensure they do not conflict with God's wisdom.

5. Dreams

For thus saith the LORD of hosts, the God of Israel; Let not your prophets and your diviners, that be in the midst of you, deceive you, neither hearken to your dreams which ye cause to be dreamed. Jeremiah 29:8

God can speak to His people through dreams but it is also possible for a man to have a dream that is not from God. Dreams can originate from God but also from Satan. Most will just be a product of our emotions, thoughts, experiences and memories, but sometimes their origin is supernatural, so we need to be discerning. Many people have worked under a deception, thinking that God has spoken to them through a dream when in reality it came from the enemy, or was simply a product of the mind. It is very important that you ensure that any dream you think has a meaning is tested against the written Word of God.

For a dream cometh through the multitude of business; and a fool's voice is known by multitude of words. Ecclesiastes 5:3

A series of life's activities can create feelings inside you that may translate into dreams when you sleep. Don't run your life by dreams without clear direction from the Bible. Do not be deceived by dream interpreters unless you are sure their gift is from God and that their interpretations line up with God's Word.

6. Human vessels

As God can speak to you through other people, so Satan can also speak to you through others.

He said unto him, I am a prophet also as thou art; and an angel spake unto me by the word of the LORD, saying, Bring him back with thee into thine house, that he may eat bread and drink water. But he lied unto him. 1 Kings 13:18

In this story, a senior prophet lied to a junior prophet. The junior prophet later died because he succumbed to the deception of the senior prophet. The spirit of deception can speak through human vessels, even people who seem like genuine Christians. It is important that you allow the Spirit of God to convince you before you start acting on counsel you have received from somebody else.

The human vessel Satan is using may be completely unaware that he or she is being used. Satan deceives them in order to deceive you. Be wise and careful when following instructions from a fellow human being.

7. Self-deception

For if a man think himself to be something, when he is nothing, he deceiveth himself. Galatians 6:3

The spirit of deception can influence you so that you walk in self-deception. This is a situation whereby you think you know what you are doing but in reality, you do not. It is the demon of deception that is putting ideas into your mind. Sometime, this demon gives you a wrong thing to focus on so as to lure you into a wrong decision. For example, it is self-deception for you to think that you have got plenty of time and thereby delay what you are supposed to do right away. It is self-deception because you don't know what the next minute will bring, so how can you be so sure of the future? If the devil can delay a good thing, then, he may be able to prevent it altogether. It is a self-deception to work on an assumption when you don't know the future.

Lest he takes advantage of us

Lest Satan should get an advantage of us: for we are not ignorant of his devices. 2 Corinthians 2:11

Satan can take advantage of situations around you to try to lure you into self-deception. He is crafty enough to exploit situations to deceive you into a wrong decision. Examples of such situations are:

1. Favour

Favour is deceitful, and beauty is vain: but a woman that feareth the LORD, she shall be praised. Proverbs 31:30

Satan can use the favour you enjoy from people to deceive you into making mistakes. He may do this through giving you a perverted interpretation of the favour you enjoy, making you misinterpret the motivation of the people who are being nice to you, and so making you respond badly towards them.

For example, Satan can tell you that the person who is being good to you is doing so because he is benefiting from you or using you in some way. This can make you start behaving rudely towards the person who is praising you or doing something for you. The more you yield to this demonic thought, the more you will start misbehaving towards the person showing you favour, until the person changes towards you and closes the door of favour. So in the end, you miss out on something good, and your relationship with the person is spoiled.

Of course, sometimes it is right to be suspicious – we should not be naïve. And sometimes the Lord can reveal to you when other people are really being deceptive. But we should give others the benefit of the doubt – i.e. do not distrust people without good reason. Actually, you may soon discover that it is you who needs them and not the other way round! Be humble when you are receiving favour.

2. Wealth

Wilt thou set thine eyes upon that which is not? For riches certainly make themselves wings; they fly away as an eagle toward heaven. Proverbs 23:5

When God blesses you with material prosperity, do not let Satan give you a perverted view of it. Satan can make you believe that because you are rich, you will never need help from anybody. He could also make you put your trust in riches instead of God's provision. It is a deception, because riches can fly away the very next day – investments fail, companies collapse, shares fall, and redundancies happen every day. We cannot rely on money.

Additionally, there are certain difficulties in life that riches can't solve. Money can't buy cures for incurable sicknesses. Riches cannot buy you genuine love. Wealth can't prevent bereavement, injuries, accidents, natural disasters, divorce, etc. In fact, riches can bring their own problems to life – anxiety about losing money, greed for more, pride and egotism, the inability to handle the power they bring, envy, etc. And of course, riches can't save anyone from hell. Riches have limitations – do not let Satan use wealth to deceive you.

3. Personal attributes

Favour is deceitful, and beauty is vain: but a woman that feareth the LORD, she shall be praised. Proverbs 31:30

Personal attributes such as beauty are gifts from the Lord, but they should never be allowed to be used by Satan to deceive. Beauty will soon fade away and other personal attributes do not last forever.

For example, Satan can deceive a beautiful woman into building her entire life and career upon her beauty. Unfortunately, when the beauty fades away, her sorrow will be great. There are many women who use their beauty to entice men to spend money on them, or to climb the career ladder, or in the case of prostitutes and porn actresses, to pay money to use them. They live their lives on this kind of venture, not making plans for the day when their attractiveness disappears.

Instead of empowering themselves through developing certain skills, such women – and men – rely on their temporary beauty. When time begins to take its toll on their beauty, they will find life very difficult because they were deceived into believing that they would always have rewards for their beauty. Hence, many are desperate to retain their youthful appearance with cosmetics or cosmetic surgery.

Do not build your life on outward beauty. Build your life on something that does not fade away.

4. Achievement

Brethren, I count not myself to have apprehended: but this one thing I do, forgetting those things which are behind, and reaching forth unto those things which are before, I press toward the mark for the prize of the high calling of God in Christ Jesus. Philippians 3:13-14

In these verses, Paul said; he was always putting in more effort in order to achieve more. He did not allow himself to be carried away by his previous achievements. Every achievement encouraged him to a better and greater effort to lay hold of a greater one.

The demon of deception can use your life's achievements to deceive you into relaxing – giving up training and self-improvement. This is the beginning of deterioration and an invitation to failure and defeat.

5. Victory

Because thy rage against me, and thy tumult, is come up into mine ears, therefore will I put my hook in thy nose, and my bridle in thy lips, and I will turn thee back by the way by which thou camest. Isaiah 37:29

The context of this prophecy of punishment of Sennacherib, the king of Assyria, is that he had boasted before God that he had defeated many nations before and so, he would also defeat the nation of Israel. But he hadn't accounted for the power of God. The demon of deception lied to Sennacherib to develop arrogance and over-confidence, such that he did not know where to draw the line.

It may be true that you have been winning all your battles, but you must accept that you are not the Almighty – you can't win every battle. Do not let the demon of deception deceive you that you are unbeatable. When you gain victories in the battle of life, let them make you more humble and grateful to God.

6. Possessing your possession

Speak not thou in thine heart, after that the LORD thy God hath cast them out from before thee, saying, For my righteousness the LORD hath brought me in to possess this land: but for the wickedness of these nations the LORD doth drive them out from before thee. Deuteronomy 9:4

When God enables you to possess what He has promised you, the demon of deception could lie to you that it is your own righteousness or ability that enabled you to possess your possession. This deception gets you to focus on your righteousness or strengths instead of the mercy of God.

If you fall for this deception, you may find it difficult next time to claim what is supposed to belong to you as a child of the Covenant. Your righteousness is never sufficient enough to give you what God has destined to be yours. It will be the faithfulness of God that will do the work for you, as a child of His covenant.

7. Favourable outcomes

And thou say in thine heart, My power and the might of mine hand hath gotten me this wealth. But thou shalt remember the LORD thy God: for it is he that giveth thee power to get wealth, that he may establish his covenant which he sware unto thy fathers, as it is this day. Deuteronomy 8:17-18

God warned Israel that when they obtained good results from their efforts, they should never attribute it to their personal ability. This is because the demon of deception can cause us to think we are in control and make us proud. While it is true that our personal efforts contribute to our achievements, it is God who makes the way for such success.

If God does not give you the grace, how do you think you can obtain what you desire through just your personal effort? To avoid such deception, give God all the glory for whatever good things He has enabled you to obtain in this life.

8. Sin

For sin, taking occasion by the commandment, deceived me, and by it slew me. Romans 7:11

Satan is the author of sin and every kind of unrighteousness. Therefore, he will always encourage you to practise sin. The demon of deception will attempt to influence you to delay repenting or to not repent at all. It will also try to convince you that a sin that attracts you is not a sin at all, or that it's OK for you.

If you notice that you can always justify your sins, coming up with good reasons for your unrighteous behaviour, then, realise that you are under the activity of the demon of deception.

9. Strong supporters

Ye have plowed wickedness, ye have reaped iniquity; ye have eaten the fruit of lies: because thou didst trust in thy way, in the multitude of thy mighty men. Hosea 10:13

When God gives you victory through able supporters, like this "multitude of mighty men", the demon of deception may try to shift your focus away from God and onto them. This demon can make you start trusting in your "mighty men" – the people God brought into your life to help you fight the battles of life.

If you notice that you are giving glory to men when such praise is due to God only, you are probably under the influence of the demon of deception. You must show appreciation and gratitude to those God is using to help you, but you must never be deceived into honouring them above God.

10. Pleasures of life

Therefore hear now this, thou that art given to pleasures, that dwellest carelessly, that sayest in thine heart, I am, and none else beside me; I shall not sit as a widow, neither shall I know the loss of children. Isaiah 47:8

The pleasures of life can be used by the demon of deception to deceive you into thinking that such pleasures will never end. If you believe this lie, you will get carried away and neglect other vital things you are supposed to put your effort into. Do not let the demon lie to you that the pleasures and abundance that life is giving you is enough.

Do not waste your precious energy on pleasurable living. We all need times of relaxation and enjoyment, but if these become the aim of your life or the things that you go to for fulfilment instead of God, you are being deceived. The more time you spend on pleasures, the less time you will have to achieve God's purposes, and it is only in serving God and others that we find real fulfilment.

2

THE DECEIVED AND THE DECEIVER

With him is strength and wisdom:
the deceived and the deceiver are his.
Job 12:16

The deceived

These are the people under the influence of the spirit of deception. Such people could be under direct deception, whereby the demon speaks lies into their minds to deceive them into certain decisions or thoughts. When they come under direct deception of this kind, they are under self-deception. Someone under self-deception will start operating under a perverted view of the situation.

Alternatively, a person may not be under direct deception but under the influence of deceptive human agents. This could be orchestrated by the demon of deception through wrong counsellors or advisers. The demon starts speaking through the human agent he has brought under his deception, who in turn is used to deceive others.

But evil men and seducers shall wax worse and worse, deceiving, and being deceived. 2 Timothy 3:13

There are people who have already come under the deception of Satan but are now being used by the same Deceiver to lead another fellow human being astray. Therefore, it is important for you to examine every advice and counsel you receive from fellow human beings. This is because your advisers may be under deception without knowing it, and Satan may want to extend his deceptive work into your life through them.

Because, even because they have seduced my people, saying, Peace; and there was no peace; and one built up a wall, and, lo, others daubed it with untempered morter... Ezekiel 13:10

This verse is about prophets who prophesied lies to impress people. The prophets were under satanic deception and he was using them to deceive other people in the land.

When a person is deceived by Satan, he becomes an instrument that Satan will use to extend his deceptive work into the lives of fellow human beings. There are many deceived advisers advising fellow human beings who are under the captivity of the demon of deception. They speak lies Satan puts in their hearts. Such people may be acting under the demon of divination or a familiar spirit that Satan is using to present adulterated truth to deceive people. You must be careful about the kind of people you listen to. Do not believe every prophecy and counsel unless it conforms to the Word of God.

And the younger of them said to his father, Father, give me the portion of goods that falleth to me. And he divided unto them his living. And not many days after the younger son gathered all together, and took his journey into a far country, and there wasted his substance with riotous living. And when he had spent all, there arose a mighty famine in that land; and he began to be in want. And he went and joined himself to a citizen of that country; and he sent him into his fields to feed swine. And he would fain have filled his belly with the husks that the swine did eat: and no man gave unto him. And when he came to himself, he said, How many hired servants of my father's have bread enough and to spare, and I perish with hunger! I will arise and go to my father, and will say unto him, Father, I have sinned against heaven, and before thee, and am no more worthy to be called thy son: make me as one of thy hired servants. And he arose, and came to his father. But when he was yet a great way off, his father saw him, and had compassion, and ran, and fell on his neck, and kissed him. Luke 15:12-20

In this story told by Jesus, the prodigal son demanded his inheritance from his father, and then went to a far country to enjoy spending it. During this time, he believed that he knew what he was doing. At this stage, any genuine advice to 'wake him up' would not have worked. Whoever attempted to change his mind or give more careful consideration to his decision would not have succeeded. This is because a person working under deception will usually have well-developed, convincing reasons to justify his actions.

However, time will always confirm the true nature of a situation. When the prodigal son had wasted all his inheritance, he had no money for food at a time when a famine struck. He had to get a job feeding pigs, just to survive, and he was hungrier than the pigs! His hunger 'woke him up'. What no adviser could do was achieved by famine.

People under deception always find good reasons to reject any contradictory advice from other people. But when time gives its verdict and circumstances clearly show that a wrong decision was made, the deceived person gives up all the arguments. It becomes very clear that it has been a game of deception from hell.

It should be noted that there is nothing wrong with a person asking for what is due to him, but the kind of spirit that sponsors such a demand is the key point. In the prodigal's case, he was greedy and wanted his inheritance early, but a spirit of deception, no doubt, convinced him that he wasn't being greedy, as he had every right to take what was due to him.

Similarly, you must be careful that what seems like a legitimate demand is not driven by a wrong spirit. It is therefore important that you constantly ask yourself which kind of spirit is sponsoring your demand or decision. This will enable you to see beyond legitimacy and discover whether your motivation is pure or if it is influenced by a wrong spirit.

Let us examine the kind of attitudes the prodigal son displayed that give a signal that he was probably acting under a spirit of deception.

1. Self-trust

He thought that he could manage his inheritance better. He had lost confidence in his father's ability to manage his inheritance for him. When a decision is taken solely because of self-trust, it raises a question about the kind of spirit sponsoring it. Wherever the devil is at work, there is always a manifestation of 'self'. It is evidence of pride. When the focus of your decision is solely on yourself, there is a need for a thorough self-examination. It is likely you are acting under the influence of a demon of deception.

2. Independence

The prodigal son wanted to be independent. He wanted to go it alone and he did not want to serve anybody. He did not want to be accountable to anybody. There is nothing wrong in being independent, but if the sole idea is to avoid being under any authority, then it raises a concern.

The devil hates being under any authority, and the fall of humanity happened when the devil convinced Adam and Eve to reject God's authority. God never created man to be on his own. God always wanted man to be under His authority. When a man is left alone, he will become easy prey to the predators—demons. If you hate being under authority and you hate being accountable to anybody, it is likely you are under the influence of a demon of deception. Hell is all about rebellion and self-rule.

3. Arrogance

We do not read that the prodigal son said thank you to his father after he was given his inheritance. We see in the story; no evidence of appreciation towards his father when he gave his son his inheritance. This gives an indication that there must have been an element of anger in the boy, which propelled him to demand his inheritance from his father. Perhaps he was not happy with the way his father was handling his business. When a decision carries an element of bitterness and arrogance, it is not likely to originate from the Spirit of God. A demon of deception is likely to be sponsoring such a decision. When you are acting with arrogance and bitterness, you are not likely to be acting under the right spirit.

4. Isolation

The prodigal son chose to go to a far country to enjoy his inheritance. He cut off any link with his father and brother. He did not want any interference from any relative. He did not value the relationship between him and his father. The son thought he would never need his father again after he had obtained his inheritance. Could this kind of attitude be sponsored by the right spirit? Definitely not. When your decision undermines a relationship, it is probably being sponsored by the demon of deception.

5. Shortsightedness

Due to the fact that his action was not sponsored by the right spirit, the prodigal son overlooked certain vital factors, which under normal conditions, he would have examined thoroughly before making his decision. Whenever a demon of deception is at work, he will make his victim have a blind spot towards certain important facts. The demon of deception operates with a veil of deception that creates blind spots all around the victim. Examples of vital factors the prodigal son did not examine when taking his decision include the following:

    A - Preparation. There is evidence of a lack of thorough preparation before he took his decision. A decision that is given careful consideration does not happen suddenly. Due to poor preparation, he overlooked many factors, such as contingency actions in case things went wrong, and how to make his inheritance multiply and so support him in the long term, instead of being squandered.

B - Personal evaluation. The prodigal son did not evaluate himself to see if he had what it takes to manage an inheritance. Probably due to anger towards his father, or laziness, he did not give time to studying how his father had been managing his business over the years. When you want to make a decision, ask yourself if you have the personal attributes required to sustain and maintain the decision and to deal with any possible fall-outs from it. Otherwise the reality of your decision will catch up with you.

C - Responsibility. If he had been acting in the right spirit, the prodigal son would have put in place structures to handle his inheritance. He would have taken personal responsibility for his decision and been proactive in planning his future.

Even if you hear God speaking to you clearly concerning your decision, you will still need to shoulder certain responsibilities. It will be your responsibility to be proactive and put certain structures in the right position to ensure the successful outcome of your action. You will be acting under deception if you fail to make a personal effort to ensure your decision is successful. Nobody can do this for you except yourself. If you fail to manage your inheritance, it will vanish away one day. Do not embark on a decision you are not ready to be personally responsible for.

D - Accountability. The prodigal son overlooked the importance of having somebody credible to be accountable to. He went to a far country where nobody knew him and where there was no eye focusing on how he conducted his business. Life without accountability is prone to wastage and losses. If there is no check and balance in your actions, you will drift into losses unknowingly. If your decision does not include accountability, it is likely to be sponsored by a demon of deception.

E - Geographical location. The prodigal son did not consider the importance of geographical location. He went to a far country and started dwelling among people who did not know him. When he needed help for survival, nobody gave him help.

Similarly, he did not realise that where you live and carry out your decision will affect the outcome of your decision. Every decision has a place of execution, and some are more favourable places than others. There are certain businesses that will fail if they are established in the wrong geographical location. If you overlook the importance of location as regards certain decisions that you want to take, you are probably acting under deception. For example, you will need to pray for wisdom if you are considering establishing a business in a place where there are currently no consumers for your products.

F - Mentoring. The prodigal son chose a far country without thinking about having a mentor to teach him about that country. Perhaps if he'd talked to someone who had lived there, he might have been warned not to go because there were frequent famines in that land. Also, he did not consider that he needed somebody to guide and instruct him about how to conduct his business and manage his inheritance. Probably if he had a mentor, he would have been told about the possibility of investing part of his inheritance for future gain.

A good decision sponsored by the right spirit, will consider mentorship from someone who can be tapped for wisdom, or somebody who can help if you run out of ideas. To ensure you are not acting under the motivation of a deceptive spirit, include mentorship in your decision-making.

G - Preparation for change. The prodigal son behaved as if he knew the future. He did not account for the fact that there is always a possibility of change, and it can be negative or positive. In the far country where he chose to dwell, famine came. There was a negative change. The change devoured his inheritance (presumably food prices rocketed sky high) and threatened his life.

The devil always deceives people into living as if there will never be a change in their situation. He makes people avoid thinking of their future and of the outcome of their decisions. With a deception that things will continue as they are today, there will be no provision to handle possible negative change; and if the negative change comes, due to lack of preparedness, the result is usually disastrous. In your decision-making, explore the possibility of change – both positive and negative – and put a plan in position to handle it.

6. Regret

Regret is always a confirmation that a course of action has been a deception and miscalculation. Regret is a feeling of disappointment or repentance. Regret comes in when a situation did not go as envisaged. The prodigal son had huge regrets. Time proved him wrong. Time clearly revealed that his actions lacked wisdom from the beginning.

The open door to deception

For the demon of deception to succeed in deceiving somebody, there are certain moral weaknesses that the person must possess that will give an opportunity to such a demon. If you notice any of these weaknesses in your life, you will need to deal with them quickly before the devil exploits them to deceive you into following a wrong course of action. If you don't, you are leaving an open door to deception.

1. Ignorance

When you embark on a mission that you know little or nothing about, you open yourself up to the possibility of deception. When the devil notices that your level of knowledge about your action is poor, he will exploit your vulnerability to lie to you and give you a perverted interpretation of the situation that you are uninformed about.

This can make you start acting on assumptions and do things you shouldn't have done. The end result is disaster. If you don't want the devil to lead you into error, seek knowledge of the subject under consideration. Never act under ignorance because, it will be a recipe for disaster. The devil loves ignorant people because they pose no threat to his destructive mission. Ignorance is his weapon. This is one reason why Christians have been at the forefront of spreading access to education around the world, in centuries past and still today.

2. Pride

Pride is an overestimation of 'self'. Pride makes you think about yourself more highly than you ought to. When the devil notices that you have pride in yourself, he will start influencing you to embark on actions with unjustified self-confidence. He will lead you into things that he knows you don't have enough ability to control. He will deceive you into underestimating the demands of your decision. He can use your previous success and victories to deceive you into embarking on a challenge that is far greater than your ability to deal with.

If you have had success in certain endeavours before, the devil will tell you that there is no endeavour you can't succeed in. If you believe him, you are on a journey towards defeat and great losses. Therefore, to avoid falling for such a lie, let every success and victory you record create more humility in you. This will prevent the devil from lying to you by exploiting your past successes. When you begin to develop the thought that you have all it takes to succeed in a certain endeavour, solely because of your past record, so you don't need any fresh effort or training, you are probably being manipulated by a demon of deception.

3. Religious spirit

A religious spirit makes you resistant to change. It makes you relate to God based on your limited knowledge about Him. You then start predicting how God will operate in your situation. Unfortunately, you forget that God is greater than your knowledge and experience. God is sovereign and He acts as He wishes.

When the devil notices that you have a restricted understanding of the ways of God, he will exploit it to deceive you into misunderstanding how God can work in your situation. Many Christians are left out of a fresh move of God because while they were waiting for God to move in a certain way that they expected, God moved in another way.

For example, a Christian brother decided not to take his sick child to the hospital because God had done healing in his life many times before, without going to hospital. The child eventually died in his house. The man was then jailed by the government. He had been deceived into thinking that God will always heal by miracles, instead of realising that God also uses doctors and medical science to heal. God can heal you without a doctor and He can also heal you through a doctor.

If you limit God to only one route to healing, you are under deception. You or your loved one may die from a sickness if you are not open to God's ways of working. It is the same God who heals, whether through a miracle or through the skills and knowledge he has given to the medical profession, as all good things come from God.

Therefore, God has the liberty to decide whether to heal through doctors or not. Be flexible in your dealings with God, otherwise, you will keep on operating under the demon of deception.

4. Sin

Sin is the practice of every kind of unrighteousness. If you refuse to repent of your sin, the demon of deception can start speaking to your mind, using your sin to deceive you.

For example, if you have not yet experienced the negative consequences of your sin, the demon of deception can tell you that you will get away with it. He will even motivate you to keep on sinning, telling you that there are no consequences of your sin. Sin opens the door to the devil to deceive you into continuing to sin, or to sin more. If you haven't yet suffered the consequences of your sinful practice, it is not that God has given you immunity against it. God gives a time of grace to sinners to enable them to repent, but if sinners refuse to repent, then the negative consequences are coming – sooner or later.

Therefore, do not let the devil deceive you into living in sin because you seem to be getting away with it. God is holding back the judgement because He is waiting for your repentance.

5. Idol in the heart

Whatever you exalt above God is your idol. Whatever you are not ready to lose for the sake of God, is your idol. Any knowledge you hold onto above the knowledge of God, is your idol. Whatever has replaced God in your life, is your idol.

If there is an idol in your heart, the devil will always use it to lure you into a series of wrong decisions. For example, if you obey your spouse instead of God, when your spouse's instructions are clearly different to God's, the demon of deception will give you any number of rational reasons to listen to your spouse instead of God. Or if there is a particular television programme you can't bear to miss, when God asks you to pray during that time, the demon of deception will give you seemingly good reasons why you can always pray later.

Furthermore, if you value your money above God, when God asks you to give, the demon of deception will minister to your mind, giving you apparently good reasons why you should not give in that very situation. It is all deception. Get rid of idols in your heart and you will close the door against the demon of deception using that idol to lead you astray.

6. Personal beliefs

Personal beliefs are the strongly held principles and philosophies about life that you use to interpret any situation around you. They silently dictate how you view life and how you act. There is nothing wrong in having personal beliefs about life, unless they contradict the infallible Word of God. If they do, then, you are open to deception from the devil. The devil will exploit your wrong interpretation of life to deceive you into an act that is biblically wrong.

For example, there is a Christian sister who believes that sinners should not go unpunished. This sister was a teacher and she never forgave any of her students whenever they did wrong. But one day, this same sister made an error concerning her postgraduate studies at university, and the lecturer refused to pardon her. The Bible says that we will reap whatever we sow. If you don't change your wrong perceptions and opinions about certain issues of life, they will lead you to be deceived by the devil and he will bring condemnation into your life.

7. Impatience

Impatience makes you always in a hurry or haste to get things done. An impatient person is not willing to wait for his or her blessings to appear. As a result, the demon of deception will send a lie into his or her mind, offering a quick way to solve the problem or achieve the objective. The person's impatience will blind him or her to the hidden dangers in such a plan.

Avoid rushing through life. Choose to be patient. Wait for your time. Pray, and then wait for God to sort a situation out for you. Do not be in a hurry, otherwise, the devil will offer you a quick-fix to your problems. And if you take his advice, you will soon discover that it has been a deception because it will get you into a worse situation that could have been avoided.

8. Immaturity

This is a lack of growth in certain attributes such as mental or moral capacity. An immature person is not fully developed to handle certain things independently in life. For example, due to immaturity, a person can find it difficult to ignore certain things that have the potential of putting him into danger. An immature person has an incomplete view of certain situations. This opens the door to the demon of deception to give him a wrong interpretation of such a situation.

An immature Christian will have limited knowledge of certain biblical principles which can result in imbalances in their theology. For example, due to immaturity, a Christian may not accept tithing as something he should do because he has only studied the freedom we have in Christ, and not the responsibilities we have to the Body of Christ and to God. This will open the door to the demon of deception to give him further wrong interpretations about giving, which will solidify his erroneous belief.

Similarly, if your immaturity prevents you from overlooking an offence, the demon of deception will convince you to fight over every wrong you suffer from people. For example, an immature brother fell out with his wife because of an insult that a mature Christian could easily overlook. The small offence was allowed to create a bigger problem. If you don't want to be an easy prey to the devil, you will need to grow up in faith and character.

9. Greed

This is a continual urge to get more and more of something. A greedy person does not know when to stop seeking more of what he wants. If the greediness is about food, he will continue to eat and do whatever it costs to have more food to eat. A greedy man is under the control of an uncontrollable urge – he will always want more and more. This kind of urge opens the door to the demon of deception to make the person blind to the danger of his actions. In the case of gluttony, the dangers include all kinds of physical diseases associated with being overweight, as well as the negative psychological effects like low self-esteem, which may worsen the problem with comfort eating.

Obesity has become an epidemic in today's society, and the fundamental cause of most of it is eating too much of what is bad for you. You must know when to say, "I am full; I don't need any more." Do not let your urges take control of you.

The other terrible greed of our age is a lustful appetite. Men in particular are susceptible to greed for sex, and this can lead to dangers like porn addiction, rape, adultery and sexual diseases. The demon of deception tells men that they can't help it, it's just the way they are, whereas the truth is that we can have self-control.

10. Selfishness

A selfish man thinks only about personal satisfaction. He is only interested in his own welfare. Whatever does not profit a selfish man will not receive his approval. He always pursues personal gain at the expense of other people's needs. The demon of deception will always influence a selfish man to take decisions that will make life difficult for other people around him. This demon will make him blind to the consequences of his actions.

If you don't care about how your behaviour is affecting people around you, you are probably acting under the demon of deception. This demon is deceiving you that there is nothing wrong in what you are doing, and that the pains other people are suffering are not because of your decision but due to their own faults. If you refuse to change, you will regret this deception because people suffering through your decisions will rebel against you and get you into serious trouble.

11. A hot temper

Because an angry man does not think through his actions before embarking on them, he gets into trouble. But he will soon realise his folly. I know of a man who got so angry that he slapped his boss at work and he was sacked. His joblessness opened his eyes to his problem, but he lived with the regret of his action.

If you are suffering from anger, do not justify it but seek help, otherwise, the demon of deception will push you into a series of actions that you will regret. When you are angry, this demon of deception will start speaking terrible ideas of possible actions into your mind. This demon is trying to take advantage of your emotional instability at this time to push you into sinful actions. So, never make decisions when you are angry, and delay making any response to the situation until you have calmed down, no matter how reasonable it appears to you at that time. Resist the urge to take immediate action when you are angry.

12. Hateful of truth

Truth is not comfortable to bear. When you hear the truth about something from somebody, you may not be happy with the person. People who hate truth always choose advisers and friends who will tell them what their itching ears want to hear, rather than the truth. This opens them up to the demon of deception, who will put false words in the mouth of their adviser. The adviser then advises unknowingly under deception, so both the adviser and the advisee are deceived.

Many people don't want to be told the truth because it makes them feel uncomfortable. Do you choose friends and advisers because they flatter you or always agree with you? If you answer yes, then you are a potential candidate for the demon of deception. The devil knows the kind of words that make you feel good and he is ready to use your chosen advisers or counsellors to convey those words to you. Do not consider something truthful simply because it makes you feel good; it may be a deception from hell. Do not hate a person because he criticises you or disagrees with your opinion. It may be that God sent him to you to deliver you from deception.

13. Poor choice of friends

The kind of people you surround yourself with could determine how vulnerable you are to attacks by the demon of deception. If you associate with people of questionable characters, the demon of deception can use them to lure you into error. If your close associates that you listen to are unwise people, the demon of deception will find it easy to speak through them to deceive you.

Do not listen to a person simply because of his closeness to you, but because of the quality of his advice. If the devil notices that you are not wise about the company you keep, he can bring people alongside you who will tell you what he wants you to hear. It is advisable to get to know the characters of your associates, and consequently their vulnerability to being used by the devil, before you begin taking their advice.

It is also important that you put certain boundaries around yourself as regards your relationships with people. This will serve as a safeguard against any possibility of wrong influence through them.

14. Tolerance

This is your ability to accept what you don't like in others or what is sinful in others. It is good to be tolerant, because we are not to judge other people, but there must be a limit to what you are prepared to endure. The devil always exploits situations to further his evil agenda. If you allow tolerance without limit, the demon of deception could operate through it by using the person you are tolerating to lure you into error or trouble. While you are praising yourself as a tolerant person, the demon of deception may be using the situation to drag you into sin or error.

A sister once accommodated a friend in her matrimonial home without carrying out any assessment of the risk associated with such a decision. Unfortunately, the friend she gave a home started a sexual relationship with her husband. Tolerance is good, but it should be done with wisdom. You will need to set limits on the extent of your tolerance. Know where to draw the line.

15. Poor self-control

Sorrow, hatred, fear and many other emotions have the capacity to control us and dictate our actions. The degree to which an individual expresses emotion varies, but what counts is whether we are in control of our emotions. Some people completely lose their self-control under emotional stress and so are prone to the intervention of the demon of deception.

It is possible to experience strong emotions while retaining our self-control, but the stronger the emotion, the harder it is to keep control. An emotional person is at risk of saying things, making decisions or taking actions that they shouldn't. Emotions can reduce or destroy our ability to make rational and reasonable responses. A person who has lost self-control due to emotion may think he knows what he is doing, but later he will realise his folly. When you are emotionally unstable, the demon of deception can create an urge inside of you that will influence your action. At this stage, it is your emotion that is controlling your action, not your senses.

A sister went to the market to buy food stuffs but when she saw a pair of attractive shoes that she had not planned on buying, her emotions jumped up and she lost her self-control. She bought the shoes but later regretted doing so. This implied that she was acting under deception when she was buying the shoes, but she thought it was her real self in operation.

It is advisable that you keep quiet or talk less when you notice that you are emotionally upset. This will prevent the demon of deception putting words into your mouth that you will later regret saying.

16. Inexperience

When you are dealing with a situation you have not encountered before or one where you are ignorant of the relevant details, you are open to the work of the demon of deception. Due to inadequate experience, your evaluation of the situation may be inaccurate. The devil always finds it easy to manipulate a novice. The demon of deception will put in your mind a wrong reaction to a situation, and because you lack previous experience, there's a good chance you will fall for his trick. Therefore, it is important that you don't make decisions independently in unfamiliar situations, but consult those who have been involved in that kind of situation before.

The deceiver

The original deceiver is the devil and he often uses human beings to advance his deceptive operations. But, irrespective of whether the devil is acting on his own through all his demonic agents or if he is using human beings, the strategies for his deceptive works are similar. When Satan is acting on his own, he operates by speaking lies into the mind of his victims in order to advance wrong decisions or actions through the person.

But Peter said, Ananias, why hath Satan filled thine heart to lie to the Holy Ghost, and to keep back part of the price of the land? Acts 5:3

Ananias and Sapphira lied to the disciples about the actual amount they received from selling their property. But when Peter announced their judgement, he mentioned that Satan was the one who filled their heart with a lie. But the question is: did they know that it was Satan who led them to lie to the disciples? The answer is definitely no. A person under deception does not know he is under deception, otherwise, it is not a deception.

Satan filled their heart with temptation by putting erroneous suggestions and ideas into their hearts. When a person is under the operation of a demon of deception, a series of untrue ideas and thoughts will be flooding his mind. The devil is speaking into his heart. Ananias and Sapphira were deceived by Satan into attempting to deceive the disciples. They were his vessels of deception, but the Holy Spirit showed Peter the truth.

Be aware that Satan can try to deceive you even through other Christians, like Ananias and Sapphira, or those who claim to be followers of Jesus but have their own agenda, like Judas...

Then entered Satan into Judas surnamed Iscariot, being of the number of the twelve. Luke 22:3

This verse marks the beginning of the betrayal of Jesus by Judas. The devil entered into Judas to deceive him into leading Jesus into a trap, with the hope of making money through it. Though, the Bible states that it was Satan who entered into Judas during this time, Judas did not know that he was under the influence of Satan. He probably thought he was acting alone. That is why, when Judas realised his folly, he hated himself so much that he had to commit suicide.

Whenever Satan influences a person into any action, his ultimate aim is to kill the person or kill others. Satan is the original deceiver. He can fill the heart of a person with lies and he can use human vessels to deceive other people.

Operations of the deceiver

As I stated above, whether Satan operates directly or through a human vessel, the way he works is very similar.

Let us examine how this deceiver operates when deceiving his victims:

Now the serpent was more subtil than any beast of the field which the LORD God had made. And he said unto the woman, Yea, hath God said, Ye shall not eat of every tree of the garden? And the woman said unto the serpent, We may eat of the fruit of the trees of the garden: But

of the fruit of the tree which is in the midst of the garden, God hath said, Ye shall not eat of it, neither shall ye touch it, lest ye die. And the serpent said unto the woman, Ye shall not surely die: For God doth know that in the day ye eat thereof, then your eyes shall be opened, and ye shall be as gods, knowing good and evil. And when the woman saw that the tree was good for food, and that it was pleasant to the eyes, and a tree to be desired to make one wise, she took of the fruit thereof, and did eat, and gave also unto her husband with her; and he did eat. And the eyes of them both were opened, and they knew that they were naked; and they sewed fig leaves together, and made themselves aprons.
Genesis 3:1-7

The account of the Fall of Mankind shows the deceiver in operation when he came to trick Adam and Eve into disobeying God. We can deduce the following from this story:

1. Positional advantage

When Satan came to speak to Eve, it is likely that he had been watching her position. It seems he came to Eve when he noticed that she was near to the forbidden fruit, as is suggested in verse 6 by the fact that Eve saw the fruit that Satan was talking about – the fruit was within view. This provided a good opportunity for Satan to tempt Eve because the object under discussion was very close.

You must be careful about who and what you draw close to. Many people have been deceived into fornication or adultery because of their nearness to someone they are attracted to. If you don't want Satan to lure you into error, avoid being close to things that can tempt you. If you don't want to eat a particular food that tempts you, then, avoid going to the shops where you will see it, otherwise, you may be tempted to buy it and eat it. This principle applies to so many other temptations. It is always wise to keep your distance from the source of temptation.

2. Secrecy

The devil had one-to-one talk with Eve. It was an isolated talk. When a deceiver comes to deceive, he loves secrecy. He does not want any other person to be aware of the conversation because, if many people witness it, somebody may open your understanding, and you may escape the deception and know the truth. Therefore, be aware of any conversation or deal that includes secrecy, with instructions such as, "Please don't tell anybody."

When someone tells you to keep everything just between the two of you, you must find out the reason for it. There are times when it is legitimate to keep something private, .e.g. a confession to a pastor, a consultation with a doctor or counselling where you need to protect someone's privacy. But if the reason is not credible, it may be that there is a hidden agenda or fact that you are not being told.

Alternatively, if a thought suddenly rises up within you that you should keep a certain deal secret, explore within yourself the rationale behind keeping it secret. Sometimes, the devil can put a thought inside you to keep something secret. It could be that the person you are dealing with is operating under the deceptive work of the devil, and the devil who sent him is trying to influence you to hide the deal. If so, there will be something about the deal that is not right.

3. The most vulnerable point

The deceiver likes to start his operation from your weakest point – the place where you are most vulnerable. In the story of the Fall, Satan started the conversation with Eve – not Adam. This is because it was Adam who received the instruction from God that they should not eat the forbidden fruit. Eve got the instruction second-hand, through Adam. Therefore, Eve was more vulnerable because she did not have first-hand information about what God said, so Satan considered Eve to be easier to manipulate than Adam.

When you are in a vulnerable situation, the deceiver likes to strike. The devil knows when you are most vulnerable and he knows the best time to send a human agent to you to deceive you. For example, you are vulnerable when your life faces a certain threat or dangerous challenges that need serious attention, so the deceiver may attempt to deceive you at such a time. Similarly, you are vulnerable when you are very hungry for certain things in life or when you are desperate for something such as a new job, financial breakthrough, healing, somebody to marry, etc.

You are also vulnerable when you are in serious need of help, when you don't have adequate knowledge about certain events of your life or you lack basic information about issues. At times like these, the enemy can exploit your weakness and manipulate you. The devil may send a deceiver who will promise you the help that you desperately need, but either the help will not materialise or there will be a catch.

For example, there are many con artists and scammers who try to relieve you of your money. Therefore, if you are facing financial hardship and looking for a quick way to pay off your debts or make some money, you are in a vulnerable position. You must watch out when somebody comes to you with a seemingly genuine business proposition – all the more so if they promise to make you rich within a day or a very short time. If it sounds too good to be true, it probably is too good to be true!

The deceiver will always try to take advantage of your needs to deceive you. Furthermore, be careful of seemingly good ideas that suddenly spring up within you, promising a solution to the problem that you urgently need to solve. The thought may come from the Holy Spirit if you have been praying for God's help, but may equally come from Satan. This is where the gift of discernment of spirits is really needed.

4. Disguise

The word 'disguise' means to modify the manner or appearance of something in order to prevent recognition or to conceal or hide the true identity. When the devil came to Adam and Eve, he did not come as himself, but as one of the animals of the garden. He came as a helper, not a devourer. He came as a builder, not a destroyer. He came with a fake identity.

Sometimes, he comes as a lover of life, not lover of death. He can appear as a healer, not as someone who makes people sick or injures them... Whatever his disguise, his plan is always to win the trust of his victims. You are not likely to fall into the trap of somebody you have doubts about. Trust is needed for you to fall as prey into the hands of the deceiver. Therefore the deceiver will fake his identity to win your trust.

For example, the deceiver must appear like somebody who is able to deliver, otherwise his victim will not surrender. A wicked person must talk like a kind person in order to win the trust of his victim, just like Satan talked to Eve. He has to build confidence in his victim. He may need to appear generous, but in reality all he wants to do is take. Sometimes, if the victim is a good Christian brother, the deceiver may need to speak in false tongues and quote Bible verses to convince his Christian victim that he is a child of God, though the devil lives inside him.

Many good Christians have fallen into the hands of fake teachers and leaders, or someone pretending to be a good Christian friend. So if you don't want to fall into deception, do not take a person at face value. Do what is called your 'due diligence' – find out what you can about this person. Certainly, before you commit yourself to doing something the new person says or agreeing to do something for them, do your thorough investigation and seek God in prayer.

Some years ago, I was deceived into rendering what I thought was the vital assistance that a Christian brother needed. He appeared very humble before me. I was carried away by his show of humility, but I later found out that he was exceedingly proud and in reality, a horrible person. It took divine intervention for me to escape the ordeal I had allowed myself to be led into, under the belief that I was dealing with an honest Christian brother.

If you don't want to fall into deception, do not be carried away by somebody's godly appearance or nice talk. Before you commit yourself, test the spirit operating behind the person.

5. Demonstration of relevant knowledge

When the devil started the conversation with Eve, he demonstrated knowledge about what had transpired between God and Adam and Eve. He started by mentioning what God told Adam and Eve about the fruit. This created a mutual understanding between the devil and Eve. It enabled them to converse with understanding.

When you talk with somebody who has knowledge about your situation, you are likely to give the person your attention. Many people have fallen into the hands of fake prophets who use demonic power and familiar spirits to gather relevant information about their victims. Such fake prophets tell their victims the story of their lives to prove that God revealed it to them. This is to win confidence. Alternatively, a deceiver with no demonic power or familiar spirit will hire human agents to gather relevant information about their potential victim, which they will then use when conversing with them.

Therefore, the fact that somebody demonstrates relevant knowledge about your situation does not necessarily imply that he is honest. He might have done a great deal of background research about you to gather relevant information concerning you.

A sister once visited a particular prophet who told her the story of her life. Everything the prophet told the sister about herself was true. When the prophet felt that the sister had demonstrated enough trust in him, he brought his real plan into action. He now told the sister to donate a certain amount of money into his ministry, if she wanted to avert a certain evil coming to her. The man also gave the sister threatening messages of evil things that would befall her if she failed to do what he told her to do.

The sister, out of fear, later came to seek my counsel. When she finished speaking to me, I told her that the so-called prophet who spoke to her was not sent by God. I shared the Word of God with her to dissolve the fear the deceiver had planted in her heart. I prayed for the sister and warned her to seek Jesus, not the 'prophet'. To the glory of God, none of the evil prophecies of this fake prophet were fulfilled.

6. Haste

When the devil came to speak to Eve, he presented the matter in such a way that she and Adam would do what he wanted them to do. The devil ensured that Adam and Eve actually ate the forbidden fruit in his presence. The deceiver always demands immediate and urgent action. He does not give his victims enough time to think through the matter and consider the truth of what he is saying. This is because if the victim is allowed time to consider the matter, someone else may come along and show the victim what is really going on.

The deceiver wants immediate action because a delay might ruin his plans. So, always be cautious about a plan that requires urgency. When you suddenly develop a thought of an urgent action concerning something, it could be the devil speaking lies into your heart to lure you into his trap.

Somebody introduced me to a business deal that required putting money into it very quickly. Unfortunately, I did not take enough time to fully consider what I was doing and put my money into it. A few days later, all the money I invested disappeared. When I started thinking about it, I realised that if I had given more time to consider it, even if I still progressed with it, I would have done it in a better way. Urgency prevents you from exploring a better way of doing things. Avoid making a decision that does not give you enough time to think through the subject before carrying it out. Be warned.

7. He begins and ends the conversation

When the devil came to Adam and Eve, he introduced the topic for discussion and he ensured that he was the first and last to speak concerning the matter. The deceiver always wants to have the first and last word, to ensure that his suggestions are followed and his deception is successful. The deceiver always wants to be domineering; he craftily dictates all of the terms. Even if a victim offers alternate suggestions, the deceiver will still try to talk the victim round to his way of thinking. He wants to ensure that his victim walks on the path he has created.

When you are in a deal with somebody and the major part of the decision was dictated by the person, you may need to reconsider it. You may need to think about why your own suggestions were entirely ignored. Similarly, when you face a situation where there is no alternate route, you will need to think very carefully before implementation. When you are being told that this is the only way to achieve a plan, think again before carrying it out. The truth is that there is always more than one way of achieving a purpose. A deceiver will try to constrain you to accept his way as the only possible one, because that is the way that will promote his deception against you.

8. Crafty

A crafty person operates in an indirect way. He will not follow a direct route because he wants to conceal his real intentions. When the devil came to Eve he started his conversation with a question:

Yea, hath God said, Ye shall not eat of every tree of the garden? (Genesis 3:1)

He started his conversation with a question, giving the impression that he didn't know the answer, when in fact he did. The devil did this in order to present himself as innocent about the matter of his deception. It was an attempt to make his victim share her thoughts with him. Then, when he discovered the inner thoughts of his victim, he would know how to attack her mind.

You must be wary of conversations that begin with a series of probing questions. Deceivers always want to find out how much their victim knows about the subject of their deception. Deceivers probe their victim in order to craft the best story that can promote their deception.

A fake prophet once asked a woman who visited him for spiritual assistance a series of questions. At the end of the conversation, the man developed a deceptive story from the answers the woman gave to him. When you are asked a series of questions by somebody you are dealing with, you may need to be cautious. Do not be carried away by a person who presents himself as ignorant concerning a deal you are about to enter into, or the subject you are discussing. It could be that he is pretending to know little about it so that you share your private thoughts or opinions, which will enable him to create his strategy of deception.

The majority of deceivers have crafty tongues. They know what to say in order to prevent their victims from detecting their true intentions.

They have a sweet tongue that is able to entice their victims. Deceivers are very creative, able to navigate their way around a discussion to move their plans forward without detection.

9. Hiding the consequences

When the devil started speaking to Eve, he only stated the benefit of eating the forbidden fruit. He told her that she and Adam would be like God, as their eyes would be opened to a world of knowledge that they didn't currently have. But he never told them that there was a price tag, for God had told them earlier that the day they ate the forbidden fruit, they would die.

The deceiver will always focus attention on the merits of an idea and be silent about any possible demerits. When you are presented with a new idea that seems to have no drawbacks, only positives, you will need to investigate very well before you start committing your resources or time to it. From my experience of life, most things that have advantages usually have disadvantages too. The majority of good plans have risks attached.

When somebody promises you that a proposal has only got advantages, you need to be suspicious and ask more questions about it. A plan that appears attractive and beneficial but omits any possible risks and challenges must be thoroughly explored before any serious commitment. Do not be deceived: there is no perfect plan or project. There will always be a hidden cost and risk. Do not give in to a false hope. Your task is to identify those costs or risks and see if they outweigh the benefits of the proposal or not.

10. He is a 'scoffer'

A scoffer is a person who treats something or someone with contempt. He is disagreeable and mocks another person over a matter. When the devil came to Adam and Eve, he did not agree with what they said God told them about the penalty for eating the forbidden fruit. He mocked the instruction God gave them.

A deceiver usually operates in disagreement with someone who is honest and good, because that person may hinder his deceptive work.

He will mock what you have been told by such a person, in order to influence you to take what he wants to offer you. He will always tell you that his idea is better than someone else's and that his option will work for you better than any other option. When somebody speaks badly of those you have previously trusted or ridicules what you have been told, claiming that he is right instead, you will need to be cautious.

When a thought springs up within you that what you presently have is not all that good and that there is something better out there, you need to be careful. It may be a correct thought, but it may not be. I know of a brother who moved out of his matrimonial home to start living with a divorced woman who had five children from another man. The brother made this choice because he found fault with his wife and believed that the other woman would fill the vacuum in his life.

After living with this woman of five children for a short time, he realised that his wife was far better than this woman. The man left her to reconcile with his former wife.

The deceiver will always tell you that what you currently have is not very good and that there is something better out there, as in the saying: "The grass is always greener on the other side of the fence." Never drop certainty for uncertainty. Do not let the devil deceive you into moving out of your place of comfort to a place of conflict. Be wise.

11. A multitude of words

In the midst of a multitude of words, you find confusion. When the devil came to Eve, he came with many words and concepts. He did not only speak against the instruction God gave, but also talked of the advantage of disobedience. He created a vision of a better tomorrow for Eve, if she would eat the forbidden fruit. He told her there was something new to experience if she followed his suggestion. He was trying to arouse her curiosity and giver her motivation to disobey God.

Deceivers usually come with many concepts and words to confuse their victims. When their victims are lost in the conversation, it becomes easy for the deceiver to lure them into their deceptive plans and capture them. When a multitude of thoughts start coming into your mind concerning a certain issue in your life, you will need to be careful before you take any action. Never make decisions while you are still confused. Clarify your thoughts first. Never make a decision under pressure from people. Deceivers are clever enough to know when they have overwhelmed you with confusion and are ready to be captured. Be warned.

12. Appears caring

Deceivers always portray themselves as if they are concerned about the welfare of their potential victims. When the devil came to Eve, he appeared to show interest in her situation, pretending he was on her side. He implied that God had not got Adam and Eve's best interests at heart, because he hadn't allowed them something good. He told Eve that they would not die if they ate the fruit – instead they would be like God. That is, their situation would improve if they disobeyed God.

This is a clever strategy by a deceiver. You are more likely to listen to a person who shows interest in your wellbeing. When somebody appears caring towards you, you are more likely to be convinced that they are telling you the truth. By giving a deceiver the time to talk to you, you allow him the opportunity to work his deception on you. You should be careful of a person you don't know who immediately shows you affection or compassion.

Alternatively, it may be someone you do know, who has previously been hateful towards you, who suddenly behaves in a caring way. This should ring alarm bells. It is possible that they have changed and regret their past behaviour towards you, but you will need to evaluate the situation carefully.

Similarly, if somebody comes to sell his products to you, but tells you that he has nothing to gain from the sale, and that you will be the sole beneficiary of the whole deal, watch out! There is almost certainly an ulterior motive for his offer.

A Christian sister got married to a brother because the brother was very caring. The woman decided to marry him solely because of his caring nature, without any confirmation from God that it was right to marry this man. A few years later, the man walked out of the marriage. Sadly, there are many people who fake being nice. Others present themselves as fools in order to achieve their objectives. It is only after they have succeeded that they show their true colours. Let God lead you, not appearances.

13. Disappearance

When a deceiver has succeeded in his plan, he will often disappear. After the devil saw that Adam and Eve had disobeyed God, he left. They saw him no more. He had achieved his objective. After someone has tricked you, he will start hiding from you. He will avoid contact with his victim.

When the devil speaks a lie into your mind, you will notice that the thought will keep on coming until you carry it out. Immediately you have carried it out, the deceptive thought will stop coming to your mind. It has done the job it was sent for. What will then follow is the regret and pain of the deception that you fell into. When evil pressure comes upon a man, it will not go voluntarily until the person either surrenders to it or rejects it in the name of Jesus. If you don't want to be a victim of deception, you will need to grow in wisdom and strength. You will need wisdom to detect deception before it matures, and strength to resist the demonic urge the devil may bring upon you to force you to surrender to his deception.

The voice of the deceiver

Now that you have learned how the devil, the deceiver, operates, it is also imperative that you get familiar with how he speaks – both through human agents and as a spirit. When you recognise his voice, you will be able to detect when he is speaking to your mind or through another human agent to deceive you.

How does he speak?

1. He speaks fear

And deliver them who through fear of death were all their lifetime subject to bondage. Hebrews 2:15

The devil uses the weapon of fear to capture his victims. When he speaks, he causes anxiety and worry. His words make people afraid. He will tell you the serious consequences of not following his deceptive suggestion.

When somebody presents an idea to you with fear and the threat of terrible things that may happen to you if you do not follow his plans, then you will need to pause and examine the idea very thoroughly. The devil loves speaking fear into our hearts to take away our courage so that we fall into his traps. When he notices that fear has captured his potential victims, he takes advantage of their lack of courage to lead them into a deception that seems to offer a way out of fear. He may sometimes promise deliverance to those he has captured with fear.

When sudden fear rises up within you, and an idea starts coming to your mind, it may be the devil speaking fear into your mind to capture your attention and offer you a fake solution. But it will only lead you into further and bigger trouble. Do not embrace an idea just because it offers a solution to your fear. Embrace an idea only when you have an internal conviction from God that it is the right thing to do, or when there is no fear involved. Be warned. Never act under fear.

2. He speaks condemnation

The devil speaks judgement. He will tell you that you are at fault even when you aren't. And not only that, he will make you feel judged and condemned. God's Spirit brings conviction of sin, not condemnation (see Romans 8:1). The devil will also give you reasons why you deserve judgement.

In John 8:3-10, the Pharisees brought a woman caught in adultery to Jesus. They gave Jesus only the reason why she had to be condemned, and did not give Jesus any reason why she should be shown mercy.

When the devil speaks, he focuses on punishment. Due to the fear of punishment, many people have fallen into the deception of the devil. He will convince them of their error and condemn them. When he notices that his victim has fallen for his condemnation, he then offers them a way of escape – which is only a further stage on their journey to deception. This is the reason why you must approach God for mercy and forgiveness whenever you sin, as soon as you are aware of it, instead of allowing condemnation and fear of punishment to grow in your heart.

3. He speaks accusation

To accuse means to complain that somebody has done something wrong. In Job 1:6-11, the devil lodged a complaint before God against Job. He told God that the righteousness of Job was only due to the blessings he enjoyed from God, so if God took away those blessings, Job would soon show his real unrighteousness.

Deceivers always find fault with something or somebody. When the devil finds fault with what you have done and you accept it, then, he will progress to offer you a better option which you will later discover is a deception. When the devil wants to destroy a relationship he will find a reason for one person to accuse the other of something wrong. If the person yields to this accusation, the devil will progress by offering him or her an apparently better relationship. Many marriages have been destroyed because one of the partners found fault with the other partner, only to discover later that their partner was not at fault at all – but by then, it may be too late to restore the marriage.

4. He speaks rebellion

A rebellious person always takes whatever side is opposing an authority of some kind. The devil calls the attention of his potential victim to what he considers wrong and how to rise against it. But if the devil is involved, it is always a deception.

In John 12:3-8, Judas spoke to oppose a good thing done by Mary for Jesus Christ. His comment seemed to come from righteous indignation – that something valuable was being wasted that could have been sold for money to give to the poor. But in reality, Judas did not care for the poor – he wanted the money for himself. And in opposing what Mary had done, Judas was putting himself in rebellion against Jesus.

The devil will speak against a plan, not because he wants the plan to be better, but to set people against each other. He wants to cause conflict and pain. His plan is that; in the midst of such dissension, he will be able to prosper his destructive mission. Therefore, if a rebellious thought suddenly crops up within you, it might be the devil trying to deceive you into a rebellion.

For example, if you are working in a Christian organisation or for a church, the devil can further his destructive mission against that organisation through you, if he can encourage you to rebel against the leaders. If the leaders are doing wrong, then obviously that should be opposed, but if you are being led by the Lord, your motive will not be of rebellion against authority, but of how to help correct and improve the organisation or church. Do not make yourself a suitable instrument in the hand of the devil. Do not tolerate a thought or an idea that asks you to rise against a system unless it comes from God. Good people make a bad situation better, not worse.

5. He speaks guilt

This is an attempt to make somebody have regrets and feel bad about something they have done. It may be false guilt – the devil loves to make people feel guilty even when they are innocent. But even if we have sinned, we can defeat this trap by confessing our sin to the Lord and asking His forgiveness, which he freely offers.

The Holy Spirit brings conviction of sin – but that conviction is only to lead us to repentance and to God's forgiveness. If we still feel guilty after we have repented and asked forgiveness, that may be a natural weakness or it may be an attempt by the devil to destroy you with guilt. If we have confessed our sin, the Bible says God is "faithful and just to forgive us our sins, and to cleanse us from all unrighteousness" (1 John 1:9). The matter is dealt with. But the devil loves to remind us of our sin and make us feel guilty again. Why? Because he can use it to destroy us.

When you allow the devil to make you regret your action, you open the door for his deceptive suggestion on how to react to your error. In Matthew 27:3-5, Judas regretted his action so much that he killed himself. The devil attacked his mind with guilt about his betrayal of Jesus, and he let the thought grow inside of him so much that it convinced him there was no way out of his mess, apart from death. Any action based on guilt is from the devil.

Avoid pursuing an action or plan that is driven by guilt.

6. He speaks adulterated truth

The deceiver will mix his own words with the Word of God. He will twist and corrupt God's words, or take them out of context in order to make them mean something they don't. He can cleverly adjust the text of the message to suit his own deceptive purpose. For example:

For it is written, He shall give his angels charge over thee, to keep thee.
Luke 4:10

The devil quoted this Bible verse to Jesus when he came to tempt him. He was quoting a psalm:

For he shall give his angels charge over thee, to keep thee in all thy ways.
Psalm 91:11

Comparing the two verses, you can see that the devil has cleverly omitted "in all thy ways" from his quotation of Psalm 91. This omission has changed the dynamic of the statement. The phrase "in all thy ways" signifies the ways God has marked out for those that depend on Him. But here the devil was speaking to Jesus to tempt him to take independent action instead of God-dependent action.

This becomes clearer when you read the Amplified Bible, which brings out the full meaning of Psalm 91:11: "For He will command His angels in regard to you, to protect and defend and guard you in all your ways [of obedience and service]". In other words, God will send His angels to protect us whenever we are acting in obedience and service of Him. If we are acting independent of God, i.e. in disobedience to Him, then, there are no guarantees from this verse that God will intervene.

The devil speaks adulterated truth. Therefore, be careful of those who like quoting statements from other people to convince you into action. Even be careful of people who are always quoting the Bible at others – don't act on their advice until you have checked out the proper meaning of the Bible verses they quote.

A Christian sister was working as a house help with an elderly woman who had many properties. One day, a brother of the elderly woman wanted to steal a machine from her house, to sell for personal financial gain. This man spoke to the sister on the telephone, mimicking the voice of the woman who employed her. He told the sister that another person would come to the house to take the machine away. But the sister realised that there was a significant difference in the tone of the man and the use of words while speaking to her. So, the sister phoned the elderly woman herself and found that the woman had not given any such instruction. The trick was uncovered.

Do not be too quick to do something just because somebody tells you the instruction comes from a certain source that you trust. Take personal action to independently verify the originality of the message. Deceivers like to quote out of context or misquote sources in order to deceive innocent people.

7. He speaks false assurance

The deceiver does not promote or allow critical thinking about the situation. He says that things will definitely work out. He covers up the possible difficulties or failure. Many people that the devil uses for his deceptive works demonstrate a sugar-coated tongue when speaking. They will give excellent assurances that things will work out if you do what they say, and fail to warn of any possible negative consequences.

In Luke 15, at the beginning of his request for his inheritance, the prodigal son demonstrated an assurance that things would work out well for him. He was so sure of his plan that he chose to move to a far country where nobody knew him. But alas, he was disappointed. The devil always speaks false assurance into the mind of his victims. When you are pursuing a plan that seems totally risk free to you, check it very well, because, you may be operating under false assurance. In this world, there is nothing like a totally risk-free idea or project. Every good idea carries certain elements of risk. It will be wise for you to explore the risk level and develop a plan to manage the risks.

8. He speaks of easy ways

Human nature likes easiness due to laziness. We generally prefer a path that demands no sweating. The devil understands that men like any idea that promises an easy way to success. When the deceiver comes to deceive, he offers quick and simple solutions. His way is always the broad and wide.

Enter ye in at the strait gate: for wide is the gate, and broad is the way, that leadeth to destruction, and many there be which go in thereat.
Matthew 7:13

The path to destruction is broad and wide – it's easy to find and easy to follow. Unfortunately, it ends in destruction, because it was founded on deception. You will need to be vigilant when you are pursuing an idea that offers a quick route to success without struggles.

A Christian brother gave his money to another brother who promised to use it for investment that would bring big financial rewards within a few days. Sadly, both the capital and the so-called gains were never returned. It was a deception from the pit of hell. Be careful of sweet words that promise easy ways to success.

9. He speaks boastfully

A boastful person shows excessive pride in his abilities or achievement. He will magnify his achievement. This is to create confidence and acceptance in the mind of his potential victim. A boastful person will only emphasize his strength and success, staying silent about his weaknesses and failures. He will never let you know his defeats in life. He will claim to be almighty and expert in the topic he is trying to use to deceive you.

In Isaiah 36, the king of Assyria sent a boastful message to Israel to frighten them into surrendering, so that he could easily take over their land – the inheritance God had given them. He was later defeated and killed. God hates people who boast, either of their personal attributes or their achievements. This is because it is God who gives us all that we are and have. Our personal strengths and gifts come from him, so any success we have should make us thank God and not boast about our own abilities. How can a man take credit for what he did not establish?

When you develop an idea that makes you boastful, you may need to pray more about it because it is likely to originate from the devil. Boasting is a work of the devil, because the devil is always trying to take what is God's. When somebody introduces an idea to you boastfully, you will need to approach the matter with caution.

A brother once approached a group of people to introduce a business idea to them. The brother started boasting about how he had used the same idea to liberate many people from poverty before. This demonstration of confidence influenced many members of the group to invest their resources into the idea without raising any questions. They all believed that the man must definitely know what he is doing.

Shortly, the man disappeared with all the money he collected from those people. It was difficult for the victims to swallow. They found it hard to believe that the man was a fake. The deceiver boasts to create confidence and acceptance that will open the door for him to manipulate his victims.

10. He speaks loudly and roughly

The deceiver does not gently discuss his ideas, but puts pressure on people to enforce compliance to his ideas. He may speak aggressively, bullying people into accepting his view. He may speak the loudest – shouting down anyone who disagrees. And he may speak rudely to people, especially belittling those who are weaker and more vulnerable.

His words do not show compassion because he has a wicked nature (unless, as we mentioned earlier, he is pretending to care in order to deceive). When he speaks, he shows no genuine respect because he himself is a very rude person. He speaks abusively, and when he speaks, people may panic and get agitated. His words melt away people's confidence and self-esteem, which will mean; he is more likely to get his own way. This is all an attempt to make people fall into his deceptive plan.

When you develop an idea that is causing agitation of the mind, you will need to pray more. It could be that the devil is the one putting the thought into your mind. When your new idea ceases your peace of mind, you will need to pray more before progressing. When somebody introduces an idea to you but speaks without any consideration for your situation or speaks disrespectfully, you need to think deep before you embark on the idea. The deceiver lacks compassion.

3

DECEPTION OF A BELIEF

A belief is a personal acceptance that something exists or is real, or is the right thing to do or way to behave. They are the principles we live by. For example, a Christian's belief that there is a God and their trust of Him make them surrender to His authority and commands about their lives. But apart from religious beliefs, human beings hold many other personal beliefs that determine their actions and reactions to situations.

Some Christians hold onto certain beliefs that they grew up with or acquired in their pre-Christian days. Sometimes, they have never considered that these beliefs may conflict with their faith. Not all life principles and philosophies do conflict with our faith in God – some are consistent with His Word. But if we have beliefs in addition to our faith, that control how we handle life's events, then, we should check that they do not contradict God's Word.

Unfortunately, some Christians exalt their life principles and philosophies above biblical standards, often without realising it. This makes them live a life of self-deception.

I am crucified with Christ: nevertheless I live; yet not I, but Christ liveth in me: and the life which I now live in the flesh I live by the faith of the Son of God, who loved me, and gave himself for me.
Galatians 2:20

This verse states that; every genuine Christian has been crucified with Christ. That is, they no longer live carnally but spiritually. But the reality is that sanctification – becoming more like Christ – is a process not an event. When a person gives his life to Jesus Christ, he is a new creation who by God's Spirit, is enabled to embark on the Christian journey. As such, a believer learns more about Jesus Christ and yields himself more to the dictates of the Holy Spirit, his carnal nature will gradually die out of him. He will be able to yield and obey the Holy Spirit and live a Spirit-controlled life.

This process is a life-long experience. The rate at which Christians will change into a Spirit-controlled life will vary, because it will depend on how fast and how much each individual surrenders the various parts of his life to the will of the Holy Spirit.

For example, a particular Christian may yield his finances faster to the promptings of the Holy Spirit than his temper. Such a Christian will be Spirit-controlled when it comes to his finances but could show carnality when it comes to anger issues. It is possible to be a Christian who will submit one area of his life to biblical standards while still keeping personal control of another area. There are Christians who are very generous but still suffer from anger. There are Christians who are very honest, never telling lie, but unfortunately the same Christians still struggle with pornography or another sin. Yielding to the Holy Spirit is a gradual progression over a lifetime.

The danger of not yielding all areas of your life to the Holy Spirit is that those areas could become an open door to the devil's manipulation. You are likely to develop a wrong personal belief from the areas of your life that you refuse to yield to the Holy Spirit. When people don't want to crucify certain sinful areas of their lives, the devil will cleverly help them to build up a personal belief system that justifies or excuses their sin.

For example, an unforgiving Christian who does not want to repent of his unforgiveness could develop a personal belief system that allows for revenge. Such a Christian will then believe that if he does not punish those who wrong him, he will be indulging the offenders in a wrong act and encouraging them to continue doing wrong to him and others. With such a belief, he will be seeking revenge against those who offend him. Such a belief system will help this Christian fellow protect his habit of unforgiveness. Unfortunately, such a Christian will not accept that he is doing wrong but even be convinced that, by punishing those who offend him, he is helping them to change.

Similarly, an unloving Christian brother who does not want to repent could develop a personal belief system that people who seek help are lazy people who take advantage of their fellow human beings' compassion. With this belief system, such a Christian brother will not show compassion on those who seek his help. The devil will be helping him to protect his unloving habit towards others by a personal belief system that is really self-deception.

This kind of self-deception has produced a lot of unmerciful Christians in this generation. There are Christians who never help others because the devil has convinced them that, in so doing, they are helping lazy people to be more self-reliant and independent, or to be more reliant on God. Unfortunately, such Christians will not see their wickedness, but instead, will boast about their beliefs, in their ignorance and selfishness. They are the type of Christians who believe that seeking help is a weakness.

Unfortunately, whatever a man sows, he will reap. Christians who deny help to others will find that they are not offered help when they need it. They will also have to pay for things that will be offered free to others, because they are viewed by others as undeserving. And Christians who are unforgiving will find that they are seen as harsh and so undeserving of forgiveness when they do something wrong. This means they are more likely to receive harsher punishments than others for the same offences.

And they found Adonibezek in Bezek: and they fought against him, and they slew the Canaanites and the Perizzites. But Adonibezek fled; and they pursued after him, and caught him, and cut off his thumbs and his great toes. And Adonibezek said, Threescore

and ten kings, having their thumbs and their great toes cut off, gathered their meat under my table: as I have done, so God hath requited me. And they brought him to Jerusalem, and there he died.
Judges 1:5-7

In these verses, Adonibezek treated the kings he defeated according to his personal code of beliefs. He believed in a punishment that involved cutting the thumbs and big toes off those he conquered. But one day a people who were stronger than him – the Israelites – defeated him and treated him as he had treated the kings he had defeated. Before his death, he confessed that what happened to him was a consequence of the way he had treated his fellow human beings.

Evidence of a wrong personal belief system

As a Christian, your personal belief system that you use to operate your life is likely to be wrong when you notice the following:

1. You are not walking in love

God is love and whoever claims to be His child must walk in love. If you don't extend help to those who need your help or your personal life belief makes you avoid expressions of love to your fellow human beings, then your personal belief system is faulty. You need to repent.

2. You become your own idol

Erroneous life principles will turn you into an idol, whereby you idolise your own opinion above biblical standards. If you strongly believe in running your life according to your own beliefs, even if they have no biblical basis, then, you are worshipping a false god – yourself. If your personal life belief originates from you and not the Bible, then you need to deal with your carnality.

3. You are egocentric

Your personal life beliefs can be developed by you to feed your ego. Some people will not accept help from their fellow human beings because it makes them feel too little. It is a feature of the Adamic nature. Such people live under deception, because while they claim that they don't take help from people, they are actually blind to the fact that God has used a series of helpers to help them along the journey of life – beginning with their parents. Stop deceiving yourself. No man is an island.

4. You live within your limits

One of the major consequences of a faulty personal belief system is that it confines its victims, making them live within the limits they themselves have set. When you notice that you are finding it difficult to go beyond your limits, it could be that your erroneous belief about life has cleverly built around you; a wall of separation from the real world in which you live. You will need to renew your mind and break out of the confinement your personal life philosophy has built around your life. Come out of the dark shadows you have allowed the devil to create in your life, using your wrong personal principles.

5. You live by works and not grace

When you operate your life with a belief system that contradicts the Bible, you will live a life of works instead of grace. Because your personal beliefs originated from you, you will constantly need to work at ensuring your life matches up to your beliefs. Instead of freely enjoying the grace of God, which happens when we hand control of our lives over to God, your belief system will deceive you to operate in works not grace. As you are incapable of living up to your own principles, because you are a flawed human being (like us all), you will soon wear yourself out and fall into depression. This is because you overestimate yourself due to the deception of your personal life belief. Many Christians who suffer from depression have allowed their erroneous life belief system to deceive them. Situations in their lives don't work out as they had envisaged through their belief system. They live a life of struggle and frustration.

6. You don't see your vulnerability

A personal belief system that has no biblical basis makes its victims blind to their weaknesses and limitations. Such Christians will fight battles they can't win because they are under a deception that makes them overestimate their strength. You will just put unreasonable trust in yourself. This will eventually land you in big trouble, because you will soon swim in a river that will carry you away.

7. You are blind to your filthiness

People with wrong beliefs will only see what is wrong with people around them, rather than seeing their own faults. They criticise everybody except themselves. This is because their personal belief system creates a veil that blinds them to their faults. They can't see their own nakedness.

8. You lack acknowledgment of God

To acknowledge God reveals your personal conviction of your vulnerability and dependence on God. A person who holds erroneous personal beliefs will only acknowledge his own efforts when he has success, especially when it comes to issues that are related to his personal life belief. For example, due to a personal life belief, some people put confidence and trust in themselves. They may believe that success in life is solely dependent on their personal effort and preparation. The result is that they keep focussing on themselves instead of involving God. But if they fail, despite all their self-confidence, such people may fall into depression due to intense disappointment.

9. You live independently

If an area of your life is not genuinely surrendered to God, you will be in charge of it. You will be living on self instead of on God. There are many Christians who live this way. But self-dependency means your life's activities are controlled by your own personal beliefs about life instead of the infallible Word of God. A person who lives on self will live a life of frustration. If your personal belief system makes you like this, you will be constantly disappointed. You will also cut yourself off from enjoying the free blessings of peace that are enjoyed by those who live in dependence on God. Any personal belief system that makes you rely on yourself is not of God. You will need to repent before it is too late.

10. Everything has to suit you

Your personal belief system will make you try to adapt every situation you encounter to suit yourself. As you are unique, it will not suit anyone else as much as it suits you. This means; you will be on a continual quest to promote your self-interest, and self-concern is the opposite of the Christian faith which puts God and others before yourself. When you notice that you are manipulating every situation around you to your own advantage, irrespective of its negative impact upon others, then, realise that it is your false belief that is fuelling such action and it is not from God.

In order to escape the possibility of developing personal life beliefs that will open you up to deception, you will need to practise the following:

A - Renew your mind continually

> *And be not conformed to this world: but be ye transformed by the renewing of your mind, that ye may prove what is that good, and acceptable, and perfect, will of God.* Romans 12:2

> To renew your mind, you need to allow the Word of God to re-programme your mind, to change your thinking pattern to that of the kingdom of God. You have to stop your former ways of thinking about the issues of life. Apply the Word of God into your spirit and let the Word determine your thinking pattern. Reject every idea or suggestion that contradicts the Word of God.

B - Grow in knowledge

> *According as his divine power hath given unto us all things that pertain unto life and godliness, through the knowledge of him that hath called us to glory and virtue...* 2 Peter 1:3

> Aspire to know as much of God as possible. Study the Bible

to discover what it says about Him and all the issues of life.

C – Submit to the ordinances of God

Submit yourselves therefore to God. Resist the devil, and he will flee from you. James 4:7

Let the Word of God be your final authority over every issue of life. Determine to live under the dictates of the Word of God.

4

DOCTRINES OF DECEPTION

A doctrine is a principle or idea that forms part of a belief system – usually a religious one, but not always.

When an individual, group, society or organisation absorb and allow doctrine to form their belief system, it controls their thoughts, opinions and actions in the areas covered by the doctrine. Religious doctrines are usually derived from a religion's scriptures or traditions, and those doctrines are taught by teachers of the religion.

In Christianity, there are many teachers of doctrine, who may be theologians or ministers of the Church, but for all true Christian doctrines, these teachers rely on one ultimate teacher – the Holy Spirit. His doctrine is biblical doctrine and it is the truth. However, there is another teacher who also teaches people his own doctrine on every topic the Holy Spirit teaches, but in every case his doctrine opposes the Holy Spirit. He is the devil, and he uses human beings to spread his doctrines.

Just as there are Christian teachers who give their lives to Jesus Christ to teach fellow believers, so also the devil uses his own trained teachers to teach those who will not accept the true teaching of the Holy Spirit, or who are ignorant of it.

Such doctrines of the devil are described as false doctrine. It is false because it contradicts the teaching of Jesus Christ.

Be not carried about with divers and strange doctrines. Hebrews 13:9

Such doctrines bring no eternal profit to those who practise them. Therefore, you must always ask yourself a question when you hear doctrines from others. How will it make you a better Christian? If it doesn't, then, it's from the devil and is aimed at moving you away from Christ.

Who concerning the truth have erred, saying that the resurrection is past already; and overthrow the faith of some. 2 Timothy 2:18

The devil's deceptive doctrines are designed to destroy the faith of those who will practise them. This implies that any doctrine or belief you hold that reduces your faith and dependence on the almighty God is from the devil.

And many shall follow their pernicious ways; by reason of whom the way of truth shall be evil spoken of. 2 Peter 2:2

This verse indicates that the doctrines of the devil bring reproach on the name of God. It means that if a doctrine makes people speak wrongly of God, then, it is likely to be a doctrine of deception. There are exceptions to this, as some of the hard truths of the faith, like the doctrine of hell, can cause non-Christians to criticise God or our belief in Him. But a genuine Christian brings glory and honour to the name of the Lord, whereas, a teacher of demonic doctrine will tend to glorify man and minimise Jesus Christ in some way.

Also of your own selves shall men arise, speaking perverse things, to draw away disciples after them. Acts 20:30

Those who practise doctrines of the devil will discover that they speak perverse things and their words motivate their hearers to rebel against the Church and against God. Such people don't speak words that edify their hearers, neither do they advance the gospel of Jesus Christ. If your words and thoughts promote rebellion and disobedience, it means you are under the motivation of the devil through a doctrine of deception. You will need to repent now before it is too late for you, for the sake of your soul.

Do not walk your Christian journey under the doctrine of deception from the devil. Do not attempt to define by your own opinion; what is right or wrong, but submit to what God says is right or wrong, for you deceive yourself if you try to establish your own righteousness. Remember what the Bible says:

For other foundation can no man lay than that is laid, which is Jesus Christ. 1 Corinthians 3:11

It means you can't re-define what God has already defined in His Word. You can't establish your own moral code or beliefs about God and still describe yourself as a follower of Jesus Christ.

Whosoever transgresseth, and abideth not in the doctrine of Christ, hath not God. He that abideth in the doctrine of Christ, he hath both the Father and the Son. If there come any unto you, and bring not this doctrine, receive him not into your house, neither bid him God speed... 2 John 1:9-10

This verse states that you are not only forbidden to practise false doctrine but also not allowed to welcome or encourage those who teach it. If you associate with those who teach false doctrines about Jesus Christ, you are unwittingly giving them credence and so guilty of aiding the devil's doctrines.

In this chapter, we shall examine some of the avenues the devil is using to pass his doctrine to humanity.

1. The doctrine of Balaam

This is a teaching that promotes compromise.

But I have a few things against thee, because thou hast there them that hold the doctrine of Balaam, who taught Balac to cast a stumblingblock before the children of Israel, to eat things sacrificed unto idols, and to commit fornication. Revelation 2:14

In this verse, Jesus condemns the doctrine of Balaam. In Numbers 25:1-3, the Israelites were influenced to tolerate and practise sexual immorality and idolatry through the counsel of Balaam. They comprised their position as the chosen and holy people of God, and were punished.

In our days, the devil is still advancing the doctrine of Balaam through various means and vessels. There are Christians who do not see anything wrong in doing what the world is doing. Though they claim to be Christians, they behave the same as the world, clearly in contradiction to God's Word.

Are you a compromising Christian? If you always want to please the world around you by copying their sinful acts, you are a compromising Christian. If you hold on to the belief that being a Christian does not separate you from the world around, then, you are holding on to the doctrine of Balaam. There are Christians who want to avoid being criticised or mocked by their friends and peers, so they do the wrong things that these people do, just in order to fit in. Such deceived Christians want to be accepted by the world and don't realise they are putting popularity before their faith. Unfortunately, the more you compromise your position as a Christian, the more you will forfeit the glory God reserves for genuine Christians. If you notice that your life situation is not manifesting the glory of God, it may be that you are a compromised Christian.

2. The doctrine of the Nicolaitanes

So hast thou also them that hold the doctrine of the Nicolaitanes, which thing I hate. Revelation 2:15

The Nicolaitanes were the followers of Nicolas. They were a corrupt sect that turned Christian liberty into licentiousness. Licentiousness is the practise of sensual sin such as unlimited sexual relationships. This doctrine advocates that everybody, Christian or not, is free to practise the sexual activity they desire. Therefore there is no wrong in adultery and fornication. Despite the fact that the Bible unequivocally condemns sexual sins, some Christians still have sex before and outside of marriage, believing it is part of their liberty as a Christian. You are under deception if you justify acts God has condemned in

His Word. Any belief or thought or imagination that produces the conviction inside you to practise sexual sin is from the devil.

3. The doctrine of men

But in vain they do worship me, teaching for doctrines the commandments of men. Matthew 15:9

The doctrine of men is any doctrine that originated from human tradition and culture. It often develops into a human philosophy and life principle, which dictates certain aspects of life of the members of that community. When people practise certain doctrines for a long time, they can become part of their lifestyle that continues even when they have long abandoned the religion or original source of that doctrine.

Unfortunately, the new generation that inherits such beliefs from the previous generation often doesn't question the origin and rationale behind such beliefs. There are Christians who, despite giving their lives to Jesus, still practise some traditions of their forefathers that clearly contradict the Bible. Such Christians are either ignorant of the Bible's teaching or believe that they can't reject what their ancestors passed down to them. Such Christians become ineffective in their witness for Jesus Christ. They are Christians without the fire of the Holy Spirit, and easy prey to the devil. They have no spiritual power to resist demonic urges and temptations.

If you hold the demonic traditions of your ancestors in high esteem, and still describe yourself as Christian, you are under deception. Unfortunately, as long as you keep to this practice, your life will not reflect the true identity of a genuine Christian. The Holy Spirit will not burn like a fire in your life. Demonic tradition is an insulator to the fire of God. If you desire to be a carrier of God's fire, you have to off-load the doctrine of deception you carry.

4. The doctrine of law

Christ is become of no effect unto you, whosoever of you are justified by the law; ye are fallen from grace. Galatians 5:4

The law came through Moses but grace came through Jesus Christ. The law was given to restrain sin and atone for sin, until Jesus came. But because people are imperfect, they were and are unable to keep God's law. When people only had the law, the devil was able to attack them with condemnation and guilt, because it was impossible for men to triumph over sin. Under the law of Moses, there was no forgiveness, because a sinner was condemned with the witness of two or more people – there was no second chance. Witnesses condemned a sinner and the devil also brought condemnation and guilt against the same sinner, oppressing humanity. It was a cycle of condemnation.

Fortunately for us, God sent Jesus Christ to liberate us from the dominion of sin and the devil. Jesus Christ brought grace, which removes condemnation and guilt. It gives a second chance, and many more chances, to sinners, irrespective of human witnesses. But despite this victory, Jesus gave man over sin and the devil, the devil has cleverly resurrected the doctrine of the law. He has developed sects and preachers to teach the same people Jesus has come to deliver, that they must still follow the law.

The devil has used the doctrine of the law to manipulate men into still holding onto the law of Moses. This means; convincing people that human effort must achieve holiness and righteousness, instead of relying on God's grace through the power of the Holy Spirit.

Those Christians who are fooled by the devil in this way see only God's judgement, not His love and mercy. Some hate themselves whenever they fall into error, and live in guilt and defeat. Others who think they are victorious over sin are boastful of their righteousness, because they believe they achieved it through their personal effort, not the Holy Spirit. They hate those they consider unrighteous and find it hard to genuinely forgive sinners.

If you are still under the law not grace, the devil is deceiving you. If you still put confidence in yourself instead of the Holy Spirit, then, you are under the law. You will soon discover that you are struggling in your Christian journey because you are relying on your personal ability instead of the divine enablement of the Holy Spirit.

5. Doctrine of perversion of grace

For, brethren, ye have been called unto liberty; only use not liberty for an occasion to the flesh, but by love serve one another. Galatians 5:13

This is the doctrine that preaches liberal Christianity. It sponsors the misuse of freedom and claims that the believer is free to do whatever he considers right, because no one is to judge others. Everyone has their own interpretation of Scripture, because the Holy Spirit is given to all, so no one should criticise another's interpretation. It sponsors an unregulated lifestyle. In churches that practise this doctrine, everything goes and is accepted, provided people are loving. Love is all that matters. Sins are excused and not dealt with. The people of God become lawless, divided, immoral and worldly, aping the world's changing values and lifestyles. All this is acceptable under the claim of liberality.

If your liberty promotes things of the flesh, it is a perversion of grace. Grace is given to enable people to put their trust in the power of the Holy Spirit instead of themselves. With grace, you can do all things because your strength comes from God, not yourself. With grace, nothing is impossible for you because the Spirit of the Lord will enable you. Grace is not liberty without boundaries – it is the power of God to enable you to obey Him. Grace is not living on self but on God. Grace leads you to look unto the Lord not yourself. A Christian who lives on grace will exhibit the power of the Holy Spirit as an enabler, because his life will be a Spirit-assisted, Spirit-controlled life.

As free, and not using your liberty for a cloke of maliciousness, but as the servants of God. 1 Peter 2:16

You are free only from the dominion and yoke of the devil and sin, but you are not free from obedience to God.

6. The doctrine of demons

Now the Spirit speaketh expressly, that in the latter times some shall depart from the faith, giving heed to seducing spirits, and doctrines of devils... 1 Timothy 4:1

This doctrine embraces all kinds of false religions, cults and deceptions, including the worshipping of images, praying to the Virgin Mary and saints, and worshipping angels. This doctrine leads men to the practice of ancestral worship, where people still commune with their dead relatives and friends. Similarly, some Christians memorise the names of angels and pray to them at certain times of the day.

All these practices were handed down to men by demons. The demons that gave this doctrine also gave methods of practising them. It is an attempt to keep man under the bondage of the devil. If you practice these acts, you are under deception. You have rejected the liberty from dominion that Jesus Christ gave you.

If you keep practising these things, your life will be under the constant invasion of demons. These demons will have the right to enter your life as they wish because you have surrendered your life to them by doing as they want. The assignment of demons in your life is to make your life miserable and keep you from enjoying the dominion Jesus has given you over demons and the devil. Therefore, you can't practise the doctrine of demons and still expect yourself to exercise the believer's authority over the same demons. It is impossible for you to reign in life with the power of the Holy Spirit when you practise the doctrine of demons.

7. The doctrine of the Pharisees

Then understood they how that he bade them not beware of the leaven of bread, but of the doctrine of the Pharisees and of the Sadducees.
Matthew 16:12

The Pharisees were a Jewish religious group at the time of Jesus, who were separatist in their religious practices and thought they had all the right teachings. In their doctrine, they preached self-righteousness and spoke only of what they were doing right, but couldn't see or wouldn't admit what they were doing wrong. They glorified themselves and overstated their achievements, but never stated their failures, and were always condemning others who they thought did not meet their standards.

The Pharisees never thought that they could be wrong. They were religiously proud, always seeking honour from the people. They also resisted change. That is why they stuck to the Law of Moses and rejected Jesus. It is a religious spirit.

You are practising the doctrine of the Pharisees if you exalt yourself instead of God, who gives you all your abilities, or never admit you are wrong, or refuse to change when needed, or go round judging others all the time.

As a Christian, you must always praise God, not boast of your own achievements. You must dedicate your successes to God, not yourself. You must not only speak of your achievements but also your failures. Never present yourself to the world as infallible, and remember that if you point your finger at other people's wrongs, you have three fingers pointing back at you. You will be deceiving yourself if you see yourself as holier than others and fail to understand that we all rely on God's grace.

8. Doctrine of seduction

Now the Spirit speaketh expressly, that in the latter times some shall depart from the faith, giving heed to seducing spirits, and doctrines of devils.
1 Timothy 4:1

Seduction is to lure a person into a practice he would not have naturally done. Seducing spirits make wrong things attractive. When a person is preaching under the influence of a seducing spirit, his message will appeal to people despite being full of heresies. As the seducing spirit is working on the preacher, so it is simultaneously working on the listeners to motivate them to believe the message and embrace it. There are teachings and messages that glorify sins, and when the weak hear such messages, they want to believe them, because the teaching appeals to their flesh – their sinful nature.

When you begin to develop boldness and conviction to return to your former life of sin, it may be that you are under the influence of seducing spirits. When you suddenly feel an urge to do wrong things, it may be that you are under the motivation of seducing spirits.

Whenever you find yourself practising an act you would not have been involved in naturally, then, seducing spirits have been working upon you.

It is therefore important that you thoroughly check what motivates you in life. Put your motivation, passion, courage and conviction under the radar of the Word of God, so as to be able to detect if a seducing spirit is working upon you.

9. Doctrine of false hope

Because, even because they have seduced my people, saying, Peace; and there was no peace; and one built up a wall, and, lo, others daubed it with untempered morter... Ezekiel 13:10

This is the doctrine designed by the devil to motivate a sinner to keep on sinning, and prevent him from seeing his wrong and repenting. The doctrine of false hope preaches peace has been achieved even when people are still fighting, or that peace is on the horizon when really it is destruction that is imminent. It preaches forgiveness without repentance.

Sinners are told not to care about repentance because their sins are automatically forgiven, and so they can keep on sinning. It is a false hope. To such unrepentant sinners; their destruction shall be sudden and great.

Similarly, under false hope, people are taught that they will reap despite the fact that they have not sown. Such deceived people keep on waiting for a harvest that will never come. Similarly, false hope teaches that they will not reap what they have sown. It is a false hope if you believe that a situation will be alright, despite doing nothing happening to make it right. It is a false hope for you to believe that you will have a different result, despite doing the same wrong things over and over again.

Arise and let the light of God enter into your spirit to remove every mark of deception the enemy has put in your heart.

5

SELF-DECEPTION

*For if a man think himself to be something,
when he is nothing, he deceiveth himself.*
Galatians 6:3

When a person deceives himself, we call this self-deception. It is highly unlikely that somebody will be under self-deception and be aware of it. You are being deceived because you don't know you are being deceived.

However, while a person may not know that he is acting under the deception of the enemy, there are signs to see that can clearly expose such self-deception and help him realise he has been wrong.

100 signs that you are probably under self-deception

1. When you expect different results despite doing the same things that bring failure. Unless you change the methods, the results will be the same.

2. When you fall in love with a stranger. When you fall in love with a stranger you become vulnerable because, you don't fully know who you are dealing with.
3. When you pursue what you don't know nor understand.
4. When you have reasons to give away the secrets of your strength.
5. When you continue in your wrongs, hoping to repent when you are ready. It is a deception to think you can delay repentance.
6. When you think you can get away with your secret faults, that nobody will ever discover them.
7. When you expect a harvest despite a lack of sowing.
8. When you think you can keep fire in your heart without being burnt by it.
9. When you think you can compete with a horse after being tired when just running with men.
10. When you believe that something good will happen despite doing nothing about a situation.
11. When you believe every thought that comes to your mind.
12. When you think those who hate your spouse can genuinely love you.
13. When you think that God will grant you immunity against His regulations.
14. When you don't know where a road ends but still follow it.
15. When you accept a person based solely on his or her physical appearance.
16. When you believe a word because of its sweetness.
17. When you keep a wrong habit but do not want its consequences.
18. When you want to pull out a mote from your brother's eye without first casting out the beam from your own eye.
19. When you pitch your tent with a troubler but expect no trouble.

20. When you consider a person who keeps on rejecting you as your lover.
21. When you think that only your life achievements guarantee your happiness.
22. When you condition your life to the depth of just your own knowledge.
23. When you believe that only money will answer all your questions in life.
24. When you want to erect a house inside another man's building and still expect no trouble.
25. When you are seeking contentment only through possessions.
26. When you are fighting a spiritual battle with only flesh and blood.
27. When you reject a counsel because it hurts your feelings.
28. When you believe you can keep your integrity despite associating with corrupt people.
29. When you believe that you will not reap what you sow.
30. When you expect your children to bring you joy despite not giving them training.
31. When you are building upon a faulty foundation but expect the building to endure time.
32. When you expect people to accept you as you are, even though the way you behave is dangerous to their wellbeing.
33. When you expect those suffering because of you to keep quiet.
34. When you demand a reward from those who receive your help and still expect rewards from God.
35. When you reject knowledge and expect the blessing of the same knowledge.
36. When you despise the source of your strength and still want to remain strong.

37. When you expect the Holy Spirit to keep dwelling inside of you despite polluting your body.
38. When you do not tarry in the presence of God and still expect to operate in the supernatural.
39. When you are using your human mind to interpret the things of the spirit, and still expect the manifestation of the supernatural in your life.
40. When your confession betrays your prayer, yet, you still expect answers to your prayer.
41. When you practise incomplete obedience and still expect the full blessings of obedience in your life.
42. When you call evil good, and good evil, and believe there will be no consequences.
43. When you keep on drinking but claim that you will never get drunk.
44. When you lack compassion but pray for mercy from God.
45. When you describe yourself as generous but never give.
46. When you claim to be holy and righteous but never cease from evil.
47. When you serve two masters and still believe you will love them equally.
48. . When you make another person responsible for your action; you refuse to accept responsibility for what you did.
49. When you expect God to place you in a certain position despite refusing His training and preparation for it.
50. When you desire a glory without being ready to pay the price.
51. When you are in poverty but still claim you have need of nothing.
52. When you claim to be religious but never control your tongue.

53. When you are sinking but refuse to seek help and still claim that you will not drown.
54. When you are walking with your eyes closed and still believe that you can never fall.
55. When you never practise what you hear but still expect the fruits of what you heard in your life.
56. When you make God responsible for all your losses, believing that God has taken from you what He once gave you.
57. When you ignore an honest and just warning but still expect no destruction to come.
58. When you use your own hands to attack your own house and still expect the house to stand.
59. When you choose the path of wickedness and still want to have peace.
60. When you refuse to honour the Lord with your possessions and still want God to fill your barns with plenty.
61. When you think failure but desire success.
62. When you fight a battle without God's mandate and still expect victory through God.
63. When you don't practise self-discipline and still believe you can never fall into error.
64. When you don't seek but believe you will find, and you don't knock but expect the door to open to you.
65. When you stand before a door God has closed and wait for it to open for you.
66. When you cling to the past and still hope not to miss the blessings of the future.
67. When you practise hatred and yet you don't want strife. Hatred and strife are inseparable.

68. When a past offence still controls you but, you claim to have forgiven the offender.
69. When you claim that you don't want war but you hate peace.
70. When you call yourself a faithful person but, you are a gossip.
71. When you never water but you expect to be watered.
72. When you are a false witness but still claim there is no deceit in you.
73. When you are full of anxiety but, don't expect it to cause depression.
74. When you bear bad fruits and still call yourself a good tree.
75. When you spoil your children, but still claim to love them.
76. When you speak carelessly, but think you won't get into trouble.
77. When you practise sins, but pray for a long life.
78. When you show confidence in what you don't know in detail.
79. When you are a quick-tempered person, but still believe you will always act in wisdom.
80. When you are idle, but still expect your dreams to be fulfilled one day.
81. When you isolate yourself from people, but still want their support. If you live alone, you will die alone.
82. When you think you can change a system that you have no experience of.
83. When you don't want the wrath of people, but you speak to them harshly.
84. When you believe that you will perform in an exercise, despite a lack of preparation.
85. When you have things of Satan in your life, but still believe you will always live in victory against him.

86. When you don't want contention, but persist with a query.
87. When you have not conquered your immediate surroundings, but you want to conquer a far place.
88. When you give your spouse a sorrow, but expect joy from him or her. A heart you have broken can't be in happiness with you.
89. When you expect your spouse to assume with you that things are OK when she or he believes they are not OK.
90. When you choose to be unfriendly and still want to have friends.
91. When you make friends with an angry man yet, don't think you will ever be the victim of his anger.
92. When you have no liberty but claim that you are not in slavery.
93. When you display your riches before an envious person, but still expect his goodwill.
94. When you are tired and weary, but still believe you can make a right decision.
95. When you subject your subordinates to oppression and still claim to have understanding.
96. When you live for pleasures and still claim to be in the purpose of God for your life.
97. When you are walking in self-will, but claim to walk in obedience to God.
98. When you have already made up your mind over a matter but still expect divine guidance.
99. When you think you can always intentionally practise sins and then come to God for forgiveness and escape its natural consequences.
100. When you are arrogant, but still expect grace from God to abound in your life.

6

TESTING THE SPIRITS

Beloved, believe not every spirit, but try the spirits whether they are of God: because many false prophets are gone out into the world.
1 John 4:1

One of the major solutions to deception is to test the kind of spirit you are dealing with in every situation. To test the spirit implies that you are able to establish the reality of the spiritual influence you are encountering. The devil is a deceiver and he uses a wide range of subtle ways to deceive people.

Therefore, if you don't want to operate under deception, you will need to explore the kind of spirit sponsoring what you are dealing with. This includes testing the spirit behind an event, action, counsel, word, dream, revelation, thought, idea, opportunity or plan. The question is – is just the natural realm involved, or is it a demonic spirit, or the Holy Spirit?

Judging the spirit helps you to judge the situation in a deeper way than what can be seen from physical appearances. The fact that something appears good does not necessarily make it godly. This understanding will enable you to prove whether something is right or wrong, and then, you will know whether it is acceptable to the Lord or not. This is the sure path to escaping deception.

Therefore, before you get fully committed to something, ensure that you test the spirit sponsoring it.

Why must you test the spirit?

1. Not every prophecy is from God

For there shall arise false Christs, and false prophets... if it were possible, they shall deceive the very elect. Matthew 24:24

As the Spirit of God can give prophecies, so also the devil can give prophecies. Therefore; hearing or receiving a prophecy is not enough. You need to determine where it comes from.

2. Not every miracle is from God

For there shall arise false Christs, and false prophets, and shall shew great signs and wonders... Matthew 24:24

The fact that a miracle happens through somebody does not necessarily indicate it is an act of God, as this verse shows. When you test the spirit sponsoring the miracle, you may be amazed to discover that it is the devil at work.

3. Not all praise is from God

Sometimes, demons can use flattery to create acceptance among believers. Therefore, the fact that somebody is singing your praises does not imply the compliments are from God.

In Acts 16:16-18, a lady possessed by a demon was praising the disciples, confessing aloud that they were disciples of God. It was demonically orchestrated praise for an unknown purpose, even though what she was saying was true.

In Mark 3:11, a demon-possessed man worshipped Jesus. It is still possible today to have demon-inspired worship to deceive innocent believers. For example, in some churches those leading worship are dressed provocatively, wearing revealing clothes on a stage where everyone can see, which suggests their purpose is not to glorify God but themselves. Every bit of the worship may appear nice but the demon sponsoring the worship makes itself known through the worldly appearance of those in such an assembly.

4. There could be tares among the good crops

For among my people are found wicked men: they lay wait, as he that setteth snares; they set a trap, they catch men. Jeremiah 5:26

It is wrong to assume that everyone in a church is of God. The wicked can mingle with the righteous people of God, acting just like them, making it difficult to see that they are not real Christians.

Testing the spirit will reveal who is who among the congregation.

5. To detect evil influence

When the devil gains acceptance among believers, he will start influencing them against God in a subtle way. In 2 Chronicles 20:31-32, Jehoshaphat was a godly man but when he started forming alliances with wicked people his heart started turning away from God, unknowingly to him. When you continually test the spirit behind your endeavour, you will be able to detect where the devil has started influencing you negatively and then take action against it.

6. It is possible for the same vessel used by God to be borrowed by devil

Do not assume that because God is using somebody mightily that the same person can never be used, at least momentarily, by the devil. In Matthew 16:18-23, the same Peter who spoke under the influence of the Holy Spirit was found speaking under the motivation of the devil just a short time later. Testing the spirit will enable you to detect when there is a switch between the flesh and the spirit as a person is speaking to you. It could also happen to you – one moment you are under the control of the Spirit of God and shortly afterwards the flesh can take over.

7. To enable you to know the real person you are dealing with

When the devil takes over the reasoning or actions or thoughts of a person and you are able to detect it, you will be in the right position to handle the matter with understanding, as you know the real person you are dealing with.

In Luke 4:31-37, Jesus was commanding the demon inside a man, not the man himself. Jesus knew a demon was acting through the man, therefore, he was not focusing his attention on the man but the demon. When you know that a person is under the influence of a demon, you will be able to deal with the situation correctly. Testing the spirit puts you in an advantageous position over the situation. You will act rightly, targeting the right source without distraction.

8. To enable you to properly regulate your relationship with people

There are people you must avoid due to the level of demonic influence going on in their lives. Testing the spirit will help you to understand the kind of evil affecting them and this will help you to make an informed decision about how to interact with them.

For example, Proverbs 22:24-25 admonishes us to avoid an angry person because such an individual can influence us.

9. To prevent the devil from taking advantage of you

The devil is subtle and clever – he attacks people where they are most vulnerable. If you are able to detect his presence, both in word and action, you will be able to act wisely against his wiles when he attempts to take advantage of you.

In Luke 4:1-4, when the devil came to tempt Jesus using the issue of food (because Satan knew that Jesus was most vulnerable to food at this time due to fasting), Jesus was fully aware that he was dealing with the devil. Jesus used the Word of God as a defence against the arrows of the devil. Testing the spirit will enable you to know the right action to take when you detect the devil working against you, directly or indirectly.

10. To detect when the devil takes over your words and actions

When you constantly test your words and actions, you will be able to detect when the devil is taking them over. If you test them against the unfailing Word of God as regularly as possible, you will know if you are no longer acting spiritually but carnally. Luke 22:3 states that Satan entered into Judas, but unfortunately Judas did not know it. Judas was no longer his real self. Tragically, he would only realise it after he had betrayed Jesus.

11. To determine the level of trust to place in a person

When you are able to know the kind of demonic activities going on in the life of a person, you will be able to determine the level of trust to place in such an individual. You will know whether to accept advice, counsel and promises from the person. In 1 Kings 13:15-24, a junior prophet lost his life by placing his trust in the word of a senior prophet who lied to him. The young prophet did not know that the man was lying and he lost his life.

Do not just walk in assumption but test the spirit to be sure of the kind of spirit acting behind somebody's words and actions.

12. To determine the motive behind every action and word

If you know the actual spirit acting behind a word or action, you will be able to determine the motive behind it. In John 12:3-8 Judas appeared to be caring for the poor, but the Bible describes him as a thief. It was only discovered later that he was not defending the poor but selfishly stealing from the disciples' money bag.

When people speak nicely but you are able to detect that the spirit acting behind their action is demonic, you will know that their motives are impure, so you need to watch out for their deception.

13. To enable you to forecast the future outcome

A prudent man foreseeth the evil, and hideth himself: but the simple pass on, and are punished. Proverbs 22:3

When you are able to detect the kind of spirit acting behind an event you will be in a better position to forecast what will soon be the outcome. For example, a marriage under demonic influence can be predicted to break down in future unless something supernatural happens to save it. In many situations, knowing the possible future outcome of an event will put you in a better position to make adequate preparation and adjustments.

14. To develop safeguarding

To safeguard implies putting necessary measures or precautions in place in order to protect you against any possible harm, damage or loss.

When you are able to detect the kind of spirit sponsoring an event, you will be able to safeguard yourself against any potential negative occurrence. For example, in 1 Corinthians 10:13, the Bible promises us a way of escape from temptation or danger. With understanding of the spirit acting behind an event, coupled with clear knowledge of the possible outcome, you will be able to plan a way of escape from the negative consequences of events. Understanding what spirit is sponsoring an event puts you in a better position to make adequate preparation and take precautions.

Do not just believe something until you are sure of the kind of spirit behind it. There are certain things in life that appear good but are not godly.

How to test the spirit

In order to escape deception, you always need to test the spirit sponsoring an event, action, counsel, word, dream, revelation, thought, idea, opportunity or plan.

To test the spirit will require the following:

1. Teaching from the Holy Spirit

But the anointing which ye have received of him abideth in you, and ye need not that any man teach you: but as the same anointing teacheth you of all things, and is truth, and is no lie, and even as it hath taught you, ye shall abide in him. 1 John 2:27

This verse indicates that; the Holy Spirit teaches us as believers. Therefore, in many situations, the Holy Spirit can clearly reveal to your spirit; the kind of spirit sponsoring a situation. While this is the truth, it is also important to note that due to human nature, we don't always listen to the voice and teaching of the Holy Spirit, and sometimes, we misunderstand. This is because your chances of hearing the Holy Spirit when He counsels you will depend on the level at which you walk in the spirit. This will be dealt with in the next chapter of this book.

2. The gift of the discerning of spirits

1 Corinthians 12:10 states that some believers are given the gift of discerning spirits. This gift enables a believer to detect the kind of spirit acting behind a situation. Nevertheless, it is still possible to get it wrong due to the fact that every Christian still has a human nature – the flesh – that wages war against the Spirit of God inside us. Furthermore, not every believer has this gift, but the Bible teaches us to "covet earnestly the best gifts" like these (1 Corinthians 12:31).

3. Spiritual perception

You may not specifically have the gift of discernment but that does not mean that the Holy Spirit inside you cannot tell you when something is wrong. Sometimes we just get "a feeling" or nudge from the Spirit that tells us that something is wrong about a person or situation. Unfortunately, according to Hebrews 5:14, this kind of testing the spirits is subject to experience. Young believers may not be able to accurately detect the kind of spirit sponsoring an event – it is something that "them that are of full age" can "by reason of use have their senses exercised to discern both good and evil."

4. The Bible

The Word of God is accessible to all, either old or young in their Christian walk, and it is a spiritual mirror, through which the real appearance of something can be clearly revealed. It creates the best platform for detecting the presence of any wrong spirit behind an event.

Which things also we speak, not in the words which man's wisdom teacheth, but which the Holy Ghost teacheth; comparing spiritual things with spiritual. 1 Corinthians 2:13

The Bible is given to us so that we may distinguish between good and evil. It is the sword of the Spirit, "piercing even to the dividing asunder of soul and spirit... and is a discerner of the thoughts and intents of the heart" (Hebrews 4:12). Any situation or event that conflicts with the Word of God has a certain demon sponsoring it. Any word that contradicts the Bible has a demon behind it. Any counsel or thought or imagination that violates the Bible has a demonic cause.

Therefore, in order to accurately detect the spirit sponsoring a situation, you will need to find out what the Bible says about such situations. What you are testing must satisfy the following conditions as you bring it under the searchlight of the Bible, if it is of God:

1. **It must acknowledge the Lordship of Jesus Christ**
   Hereby know ye the Spirit of God: Every spirit that confesseth that Jesus Christ is come in the flesh is of God: And every spirit that confesseth not that Jesus Christ is come in the flesh is not of God: and this is that spirit of antichrist, whereof ye have heard that it should come; and even now already is it in the world. 1 John 4:2-3

   Every situation that is of the Spirit of God must acknowledge the Lordship of the Lord Jesus Christ. This implies that; such a situation must surrender to the will of God. The devil will never say: "Lord, let Your will be done." So, any plan or project that is devised by an organisation, group or individual that is not ready to surrender to God's will, can never be of God. A plan can look 'good' and seem morally right, but the devil sometimes comes as an angel of light.

   Therefore, you are likely to be under deception if your situation can't surrender to the will of God. For example, if God closes a door, and you are struggling to open the same door, you are under demonic influence.

2. **It must agree totally with the Word of God**
   When a situation is only partially in line with the Word of God or does not agree with the Word of God at all, then the devil is sponsoring it.

   In Matthew 4:6, Satan quoted Psalm 91:11 – but omitting an important part of the verse. If your situation partially fits with the Word of God, but an essential part of the text is ignored or contradicted, Satan is sponsoring it. For example, if you pay a tithe of five per cent of your wage instead of the ten per cent the Bible commands, you are acting under the deception of the devil. Though you have paid your tithe as commanded by the Word of God, but you have not paid the full percentage required.

3. **It must exalt God not self**
   Luke 4:8 makes it clear that only God should be worshipped. Therefore, if you do something with the aim of showing that you are better than somebody else, you are exalting self and it can never be of God. As a Christian, you are to only pursue the praise of God, not yourself.

4. **It must be capable of bearing good fruits**
   If the outcome of the situation will only bear bad fruit, then it is unlikely to be sponsored by the Spirit of God. Matthew 7:16-20 explains that a tree is known by its fruits. The spirit that advances destruction can never be under the sponsorship of the Spirit of God. For example, if your plan will break the heart of your spouse, it is the devil influencing you.

5. **It must derive its source from God**
   A situation under the sponsorship of the Spirit of God derives its survival from the Spirit of God. If such a situation is fuelled by human strength, it is likely to be sponsored by the devil. This is because if the situation turns out well, it will not glorify God but those that fuelled it. Isaiah 26:4 admonishes us to put our trust in God for His strength. Whatever is contrary to this is false. Therefore, you may need to ask yourself a question: who will fuel your plan?

6. It must not promote a tradition of men that is contrary to the Bible

According to Mark 7:13, the traditions of the Pharisees nullified the Word of God. Therefore, if a tradition of your culture or church denomination undermines the Word of God, it is under the sponsorship of the devil.

7. It must not feed your ego

A situation that will make you proud instead of being humble, is likely to have the devil behind it. James 4:16 says that boasting of our own achievements is evil. The devil makes people boastful but God makes people humble. Therefore, if your plan will feed your ego, a demon is likely to be the sponsor of it.

8. It must not bring confusion

1 Corinthians 14:33 states that God is not the author of confusion. The devil is the one who causes confusion and fear. If the situation you are testing causes you to be afraid and confused, it is very likely that the spirit sponsoring it is not of God. If the fear persists, it is advisable for you to drop the plan.

9. It must not add sorrow to sorrow

The Spirit of the Lord brings comfort. He does not add sorrow to sorrow. The Holy Spirit removes pain, worry, anxiety and discouragement. The devil acts in the opposite direction. Acts 9:31 says that the Holy Spirit brings comfort, and in John 14:16 Jesus refers to the Holy Spirit as 'Comforter'. Therefore, if your situation promotes discomfort, then you need to take caution because it is likely that devil is acting behind the scenes in some way.

10. It must not contradict past prophecy

In 1 Kings 13:15-18, a young prophet received a prophecy from a senior prophet which was contrary to the prophecy he personally received from God. Unfortunately for this young prophet, he chose to believe the contrary prophecy of the senior prophet which was a deception. He eventually lost his life. If you receive a new prophecy that contradicts a past prophecy you once received from God, you will need to pause and investigate the situation further. It may be that the devil is at work.

11. It must not advance instability

Proverbs 24:21 warns us against people who are "given to change" – those who are always rebelling against something or never commit to anything for very long. People seek unending change because they lack satisfaction. If you notice that you don't stay for a long time in a job, career, location, relationship, etc., then, it is likely that the devil is the one sponsoring it. This is because instability contradicts the Word of God that promises us stability, e.g. Ephesians 4:14.

12. It must not require negative moral adjustment

Therefore to him that knoweth to do good, and doeth it not, to him it is sin. James 4:17

If fitting into a situation demands that you drop certain godly attributes, then, it is clear that the spirit at work is not of God. Also, a situation that requires you to commit the sin of omission – that is, deciding to not do something good that you know you should do – cannot be of God. For example, if you have to avoid telling the truth in order to gain an advantage for yourself or your work, then the devil is certainly sponsoring the situation.

13. It must not isolate you from any responsibility

A situation that indicates that you have no role to play in order for success to happen is likely to be a deception. Whatever you want to do in life, you will always have personal responsibility for it. It is a deception to expect that God should do everything for you. After Paul's dramatic conversion on the road to Damascus, according to the King James Version of Bible, almost the first thing he did was ask: "Lord, what wilt thou have me to do?" James 2:22 teaches that our faith is made complete by our actions.

14. It must not bring another yoke

A situation that will enslave you is wrong and is likely to have the devil acting behind it. For example, if you are offered a solution that could lead to addiction or back into a sin that you have overcome or a temptation you have a weakness towards, then, the devil is at work. And a project or idea that requires you to be more committed to it than to church, family or spouse is a deception. Jesus said in Matthew 11:30 that; his yoke is light and easy. He does not complicate the lives of his followers, and he doesn't enslave them.

15. It must not be casual on wrong things

Any situation that treats sins or abnormal things casually is likely to be encouraging them, and it is likely to be from the devil. When you are being told that a minor insult or a little lie does not really matter, you need to start suspecting the devil to be at work. In the sight of God, every wrong thing – no matter the size – is considered a serious issue, because little things can grow.

Galatians 5:9 states that "a little leaven leaveneth the whole lump". In other words, a little wrong thing can grow in size and influence until it becomes something much worse. In testing the spirit behind a situation, do not ignore the wrong things that seem to be minor.

16. It must not breed unhealthy argument

2 Timothy 2:23-24 advises that we should not get involved in unhealthy arguments. This is because foolish arguments can become a breeding ground for insult, offence and every kind of emotional damage. If some situation you are involved in promotes unnecessary and unhelpful arguments, you should refrain from such arguments and possibly from all your involvement in the situation, because the devil is likely to be at work. He likes to cause arguments between people, so that he can use the situation to manipulate their emotions and cause offence and antagonism.

17. It must not create disunity

If your situation promotes disunity between yourself and your spouse or other people, then, the devil is likely to be trying to set people against each other. The Spirit of God does not cause discord and conflict. If God has given you a plan or idea that causes dissent, it is because the devil has raised opposition to it.

But it is also possible that the plan or idea itself is not from God, if it is causing tension. Romans 16:17 advises Christians to avoid people who cause division. In testing the spirit sponsoring your situation, any evidence of disunity, particularly among Christians, could be a confirmation that the devil is acting behind the scene.

18. It must not deny God's power

The devil will never acknowledge the power of God even if the evidence is overwhelming. In many situations where Jesus performed miracles, the devil influenced people to attack Jesus, saying that he was using demonic powers. The devil will try to deny the power of God so that he can claim the glory due to God.

When your situation will promote the denial of God's power, it is clearly from the devil. When what God is doing is attributed to a demonic movement, then, the devil is the sponsor of such accusations. 2 Timothy 3:5 reveals that there are people who seem to be Christians who deny the power of God, so they should be avoided. And if you think or proclaim that it is your ability, not the power and mercy of God that has given you certain victories, you are under the motivation of the devil – who is probably acting through your pride.

19. It must not speak evil of God

In Genesis 3:4-5, the devil came to Adam and Eve to fault God. The devil is still using the same strategy today. He likes to speak evil of God. He can speak into the mind of people to start blaming God, finding fault with God and discrediting the things of God. Whatever makes you blame or question or fault God is of the devil; that is the devil speaking into your mind.

20. It must not melt your faith

A situation that will lead you to unbelief or doubting God is of the devil. Whatever will cause a reduction of your faith in God cannot be of God. In 1 Timothy 6:20-21, Paul advises Timothy to avoid certain things that could make him fall into errors concerning the faith. There are false teachings that are capable of making Christians unknowingly move into wrong doctrines or even to lose their faith. Therefore, if something comes along that is capable of damaging your faith, you must know that the devil is acting behind the scenes to destroy your relationship with God.

21. It must not lead to idolatry

1 John 5:21 teaches us to avoid idols. An idol is anything that replaces God in your life, any situation that occupies the position of God in your life. For example, if your business or career takes priority over God in your life, it is your idol. If your spouse or children are more important to you than God, they are your idols. As a Christian, you must love God above every other thing or person. It is the devil who makes you give your heart to a thing or person above God. So if you notice that something in your life is becoming more important than God, then, you are moving into idolatry and the devil is behind it.

22. It must not advance another doctrine

If your situation leads you into believing a doctrine that is not in total agreement with the Bible, the devil is likely to be the sponsor of it. 2 John 1:10 states that; we should not allow a contrary doctrine into our lives. Therefore, if your situation involves a doctrine that is contrary to the Bible, it is a clear indication that the devil is sponsoring it.

It is important to realise that the kind of person or source of a doctrine does not determine its validity. Even some of the greatest Bible teachers, pastors and theologians have taught false things. As long as it is contrary to the Bible, such a doctrine must not be accepted – irrespective of the status or knowledge of the person who established it. Be wise.

23. It must not be seductive

The devil is a seducer, making people act in a way that they would not naturally act were it not for his influence. If you feel this is what is happening to you, then the devil is likely to be involved. 1 Timothy 4:1 confirms that one of the signs of the end times is that; people will fall into the trap of seductive spirits. Therefore, you should start suspecting the devil if your situation is making you act in a way you normally wouldn't.

24. It must not place pressure on you
The devil likes to pressurise people in order to force them to do his will. But God will always respect your free will in all situations. Hebrews 12:16-17 tells us that Esau sold his birth right due to pressure of hunger. In 1 Samuel 13:10-12, King Saul acted under pressure to do what he was not supposed to do as a king. Any situation that pressurises you to act in a certain way is not likely to be of God.

25. It must not cease your peace
According to John 14:27, one of the legacies Jesus left for us is his divine peace. So if your situation or a decision is making your heart troubled, it is likely that it is not of God; the devil may be at work. We can be in the most troubling circumstances, yet if we are making the right decision or taking the right path, we will know God's peace. But if in your heart; you do not feel right about something, ask God why you have a lack of peace. If you don't experience peace of mind and heart in your situation, begin to suspect that the devil is at work in some way. Ask the Holy Spirit to reveal what the problem is.

26. It must not be of self-focused but God-focused
In Isaiah 14:13-14 the devil uses the word 'I' five times in two sentences. His focus is on himself as the executioner of his own plans. When the Holy Spirit is speaking through a person, He speaks in the acknowledgement of the sovereignty of God. Therefore, examine your motives and see if you and your needs are always at the centre of your plans. If you notice that you are doing things for your own advantage, at the expense of others, then you need to change and it is possible that the devil has been at work.

27. It must not glorify a problem
A situation that glorifies the problem only speaks of the problem and fails to offer solutions. When God speaks of a problem, He

offers a solution to it. He makes us aware of sin and mistakes in order to help us overcome those things. But when the devil speaks of problems, he will be silent about the solution. This is an attempt to make the receiver of such a message descend into anxiety, guilt, confusion or fear – exacerbating the problem rather than solving it.

God never puts His people in limbo. He always provides a way out, if we will choose it. In Joshua 7:11-15, God spoke to Joshua about the problem in the camp of Israel and offered a solution. When your situation puts you into a darkness with no light at the end of the tunnel, it may be the devil at work.

28. It must not dictate the move of the Holy Spirit

The devil makes people attempt to determine the spiritual atmosphere that suits their desires. Such people want to fix spiritual things by themselves. They will not allow the Spirit of God to move to bring glory to the name of God, but rely on their own understanding and resources. In Isaiah 30:10, the Bible says that rebellious people told the prophets what they should prophesy. They wanted to fix spiritual things by themselves.

When your situation will not allow the free flowing of the Spirit of God, then it is the devil that is at work in such a place. For example, if you won't listen to counsellors who say things you don't like and you only want to hear what suits you, then you are under the deception of the devil.

29. It must not take you beyond your limit

1 Corinthians 10:13 states that God will not allow us to be tempted beyond what we can endure, and will always provide a way of escape. He will not put us in a situation that will break our strength. Therefore, if you find yourself under a challenge that you can't bear, and there seems to be no way to resist the temptation, it is likely that the devil is at work. Do not attribute to God, the challenges that break your strength. God will not put you in such a situation because He knows your limits. It is the devil who leads us into traps – but God can show you how to overcome temptation.

30. It must not promote earthly repentance

2 Corinthians 7:10 reveals two types of repentance: the human kind that leads to death and the heavenly sort that leads to life. It is earthly, human repentance if it breeds the 'sorrow' of self-hatred, guilt, self-condemnation, etc. In fact, it is not real repentance – it is just sorrow that we have been found out, or that we are suffering the consequences of our sin – rather than a real desire to change. It is the devil who promotes this kind of repentance, which is really just regret and shame. If the Holy Spirit leads us to true repentance, it will end in forgiveness, freedom and hope.

It is right to regret our mistakes, to hate what we have done wrong, but it is not right for you to hate yourself. Furthermore, earthly repentance is never real because it not lasting. Someone who is merely regretting rather than truly repenting will be like a dog that returns to its vomit – he will do the wrong thing again. Therefore, if you notice that your repentance is never permanent and it destroys your self-esteem, then, the devil is likely to be at work.

Grow in the knowledge of God

Finally, in your effort to test the spirits, make a positive choice to grow up in the knowledge of God. Regularly study the Word of God and allow its authority in your situation to be final. Store the Word of God in your spirit continually, and abide in Christ Jesus always.

Avoid taking a Bible verse out of context in order to make it fit into your situation. Furthermore, avoid interpreting the Bible using your tradition or culture. When reading the Bible, check cross-references – that means comparing with other verses on the same subject, in order to gain a wider and deeper knowledge of the Word of God. Do not break a verse in the Bible by taking just a part of it to justify your situation. Surrender your situation to the totality of the Word of God.

Use the Bible as a defensive weapon in all your situations. Grow in faith in God and always be alert. Be a Christian who builds his trust in God's Word. Believe what you read in the Bible and practise and confess it into your situation. Meditate regularly on the Word and know that what it says is settled for ever in heaven. It is not subject to human interpretation or understanding. Human beings may misinterpret it but that does not change what it really means – the Word of God never changes. Make it your objective to understand the Word correctly, not just by extensive study but by asking for the help of the Holy Spirit.

Live a life of faith in God. Whatever the situation, be assured that God is always with you. Watch out for your influencers – things or people that influence your decisions or words. Try to surround yourself with good influencers.

Before you accept any information or revelation, compare and contrast it with the Word of God, and if there is deviation from the Word, reject it. As a Christian, avoid a quick-fix mentality. Many good people fall into deception because they want to find a quick solution to their situation. Stop seeking miracles but seek the Miracle Worker – we seek God for who He is, not for what He can do for us.

Always seek the truth of Jesus Christ. It is the only truth, and the truth that sets us free. Surrender yourself to Word of God, so that you are moulded by it, rather than by the world. Avoid justifying your mistakes. Be quick to accept your faults when the Bible shows that it is you at fault. Let the Holy Spirit help you to rise above carnality; subject your flesh to holy discipline. Get rid of your old way of reasoning. Renew your mind using the Word of God.

Guard your emotions, because they can make you vulnerable to deception. Make a conscious effort to rule over your emotions. Do not allow external forces to gain control of your reaction to situations; always put yourself under the calmness of the Holy Spirit.

Avoid trusting what you have not tested and proved to be right biblically. Be sure of your facts and figures. Don't be gullible.

7

WALKING IN THE SPIRIT

*This I say then, Walk in the Spirit,
and ye shall not fulfil the lust of the flesh.*
Galatians 5:16

In order to escape the deception of the enemy, you will need to be a person who walks in the Spirit in all situations that come your way.

To walk in the Spirit means to be always led by the Spirit of God, living under His influence and constantly obeying His directions.

When you start walking in the Spirit, you will no longer fulfil the lusts of the flesh nor follow the temptations of this world. As a person walking in the Spirit, your thoughts, motivation, passion, ambition and actions will be fully controlled by the Holy Spirit who lives inside you.

The Holy Spirit knows all things – including the visible and invisible. When you submit to His guidance in all situations, you will not fall into deception. Deception by definition means; you are not aware of the deception, but with the all-knowing Holy Spirit inside you, it is possible to become aware of deceptions and so avoid them. The Spirit will direct you, provided you listen to Him and submit to Him.

Walking in the Spirit is a sure way to a life of victory over every demonic manipulation in this world.

We fall into deception when we walk out of the leading of the Spirit of God.

For the flesh lusteth against the Spirit, and the Spirit against the flesh: and these are contrary the one to the other: so that ye cannot do the things that ye would. Galatians 5:17

This verse indicates that; there is a constant war between our flesh and spirit. When you desire to do the will of God through the touch of the new spirit you received when you first became born again, your flesh will attempt to hinder you. Therefore, a person walking in the Spirit is victorious over the flesh. If you are walking in step with the Spirit, in every situation where the flesh tries to influence you, you are able to defeat it. This victorious life is only possible when you walk in the Spirit.

In reality, walking in the Spirit can only be effective if certain disciplines are followed. Therefore, to help you walk in the Spirit effectively, the following tips have been developed. I believe that if you carefully observe them, it will become a natural and normal thing for you to walk in the Spirit.

1. Walk with a new mind

The mind of the flesh is different from that of the Spirit of God. The way you thought and acted before you became a Christian has to change. You have to develop another mindset which is called the mind of Christ (1 Corinthians 2:16). It is this new mind that will change your thinking, imagination, meditation, belief system, and then change your actions.

And be not conformed to this world: but be ye transformed by the renewing of your mind, that ye may prove what is that good, and acceptable, and perfect, will of God. Romans 12:2

A renewed mind is a mind that thinks biblically. Therefore, you will need to continually input the Word of God into your mind in order to re-programme how your mind functions.

When your mind has been fully renewed, it will think differently. It will think only things that fall within the parameters of the virtues listed in this verse:

Finally, brethren, whatsoever things are true, whatsoever things are honest, whatsoever things are just, whatsoever things are pure, whatsoever things are lovely, whatsoever things are of good report; if there be any virtue, and if there be any praise, think on these things. Philippians 4:8

2. Walk in the light of His Word

For the word of God is quick, and powerful, and sharper than any twoedged sword, piercing even to the dividing asunder of soul and spirit, and of the joints and marrow, and is a discerner of the thoughts and intents of the heart. Hebrews 4:12

The light of God brings illumination and understanding. You will escape deception if you chose to always bring your situation into the light of God. That is, you seek understanding of your situation in accordance with the Word of God. Whatever you want to do or say, you must ensure that it agrees with the Word of God. Let the Word interpret it and shape it. Do not let the world interpret the situation for you because the world's views are corrupted by the enemy. For example, what the Bible describes as evil, the world may say is good.

3. Walk in humility

Let this mind be in you, which was also in Christ Jesus: Who, being in the form of God, thought it not robbery to be equal with God: But made himself of no reputation, and took upon him the form of a servant, and was made in the likeness of men: And being found in fashion as a man, he humbled himself, and became obedient unto death, even the death of the cross. Philippians 2:5-8

Pride is the sure path to deception. Jesus was never deceived because he was very humble in all his ways. Humility makes you teachable. If you can be humble in all your ways, the Spirit of God will constantly keep you informed of the reality of your situation so that; you will not fall into deception.

4. Walk before God always

And when Abram was ninety years old and nine, the LORD appeared to Abram, and said unto him, I am the Almighty God; walk before me, and be thou perfect. Genesis 17:1

God told Abram to walk before Him, which means to live a life of total obedience to God which would make him blameless. Obedience makes it possible for the Spirit of God to lead and direct your steps. Decide to give God your total attention in all your ways. Obey God totally in all that you do.

5. Walk with a different spirit

You must actively choose to be different to the spirit of the world. It is impossible to believe by the Spirit and still reason and think the way the world does.

But my servant Caleb, because he had another spirit with him, and hath followed me fully, him will I bring into the land whereinto he went; and his seed shall possess it. Numbers 14:24

Caleb thought and spoke differently from the majority. To walk in the Spirit will require you to be different from the majority of people around you. Do not follow the crowd just because they are many. Stick to what the Word of God says, irrespective of the level of opposition. If you can practise this, you will escape the deception that will befall those in the world.

6. Walk with caution

As a Christian, do not be care-free. The Bible teaches us not to worry, but it also teaches us to be alert. People fall into deception because they are careless and don't pay attention to potential pitfalls. To walk in the Spirit, you have to walk with caution, and do not enter into what the Holy Spirit has told you not to do. Being alert to spiritual danger will help you detect the subtle way the enemy deceives people.

See then that ye walk circumspectly, not as fools, but as wise.
Ephesians 5:15

A fool never learns from experience, and he is not cautious. If you are in doubt about the right thing to do, ask the Holy Spirit to give you a clear instruction concerning your situation. Do not operate on assumptions.

7. Walk in freedom

Part of the strategy of the enemy to keep people in bondage is the use of the weapons of guilt, condemnation and self-pity. These produce constraints that will not let you exercise your rights as a child of God, under certain situations. Walking in the Spirit will require that you exercise your liberty as a Christian. Because of the blood of Christ, you are at liberty to do what the Holy Spirit wants you to do.

Stand fast therefore in the liberty wherewith Christ hath made us free, and be not entangled again with the yoke of bondage. Galatians 5:1

If you allow the devil to shake your liberty, he will drag you into deception.

8. Walk in boldness

It will require boldness to refuse to compromise your position in the face of negative popular opinion. Walking in the Spirit involves operating in the boldness of the Holy Spirit. A man under the spirit of fear will not be able to hear clearly from the Spirit of God. You will need to be courageous when you face opposition and confrontation. Fear enables the devil to drag you into deception.

And now, Lord, behold their threatenings: and grant unto thy servants, that with all boldness they may speak thy word. Acts 4:29

In order not to compromise their work for the Lord, the disciples prayed to God for boldness. If necessary, ask God for boldness so that you can confidently resist the devil's attempts to cower you into submission to his deceptions.

9. Walk in peace

In the absence of peace, there is anxiety. It is impossible to walk in the Spirit under anxiety and worry.

These things I have spoken unto you, that in me ye might have peace. In the world, ye shall have tribulation: but be of good cheer; I have overcome the world. John 16:33

Jesus assured us of our victory over the world and all its wickedness. Even though He said we will have troubles, his assurance was given to strengthen our mind, so we can be at peace in all situations. When people lose inner peace they become vulnerable to being taken captive by the enemy. A man who has no peace will enter into deception unwittingly. To be led by the Spirit of God will require holding onto your peace in all situations, so that you can perceive the Holy Spirit's guidance when He gives it.

10. Walk in faith

Faith dispels fear. Walking in the Spirit will require faith, because you will need it to be able to trust God when He asks you to do something in difficult circumstances. No matter how hard a situation may be, our God is able to subdue it. Therefore, you will need to exercise faith in God by trusting Him in all situations. This will keep you stable and prevent the devil from taking advantage of your situation to deceive you.

For we walk by faith, not by sight. 2 Corinthians 5:7

When you walk in faith, you will not be controlled by what you see but, what you believe. This will stop the enemy deceiving you.

11. Walk unnaturally

But the natural man receiveth not the things of the Spirit of God: for they are foolishness unto him: neither can he know them, because they are spiritually discerned. 1 Corinthians 2:14

A natural man operates his life with just his senses; he interprets situations naturally. A Christian is born again into the world of the supernatural, where anything is possible. To walk in the Spirit will require that you cease being natural both in your thinking and expectations.

You will be open to deception if you only walk in the natural. This is because the devil likes to deceive us into using our senses to interpret the situations and circumstance of life, when sometimes, we need a spiritual – or unnatural – perspective. Be unnatural in your thinking. Focus on the supernatural move of God in all your situations. Know that miracles do happen, but it requires unnatural thinking to believe and expect for them.

12. Walk in the quietness of the Spirit

Walking in the Spirit requires a quietness of the spirit. This is because you will need to be silent in order to hear the Holy Spirit, because He speaks in a gentle, small voice.

And after the earthquake a fire; but the LORD was not in the fire: and after the fire a still small voice. 1 Kings 19:12

God spoke to Elijah with a still, small voice. Unless he was quiet in his spirit, it would have been impossible for him to hear what God was saying to him through the Spirit. An agitated mind will only hear from the voice of the flesh, which will lead to deception. In all situations, keep your emotions under control and don't let them rule and dictate to you.

13. Walk in love

To walk in love implies that you derive your motivation from love in whatever you do. Let love be your driving force behind every action. Give in love, counsel in love, help in love, speak in love, think in love, etc. It is impossible to be led by the Holy Spirit when you are full of bitterness and unforgiveness.

Beloved, let us love one another: for love is of God; and every one that loveth is born of God, and knoweth God. 1 John 4:7

God is love and whoever claims to be led by the Spirit must operate in love. Without love as a motivation, you will be walking in deception.

14. Walk worthy of the Lord

That ye might walk worthy of the Lord unto all pleasing, being fruitful in every good work, and increasing in the knowledge of God... Colossians 1:10

To walk worthy of the Lord will require a fruit-bearing life. This is a life that is evident of walking in the Spirit. When you live a life that brings praise and honour to the Lord, the deceiver will naturally flee from your life because the good fruits you are bearing intimidate him. Therefore, a fruit-bearing life is an antidote to deception because it drives away the deceiver.

15. Walk in the newness of life

Therefore we are buried with him by baptism into death: that like as Christ was raised up from the dead by the glory of the Father, even so we also should walk in newness of life. Romans 6:4

The new life you were given when you were born again is a life that shows the nature of God, your Saviour. It is a life of holiness. When you choose to live holy, the Holy Spirit will be able to give you guidance in all your affairs and so, you will not be deceived. Be holy and the deceiver will be far away from your life. God bless you indeed, in Jesus' name. Amen

BOOKS FROM THE SAME AUTHOUR

Journey to the Next Level

The New Creature

Building a Glorious Home:
A Pathway to a Successful Marriage

Words That Heal

The Enemy of Marriage

The Winning Formula

Faith that Always Wins:
Discover the Power of a Living Faith

Common Mistakes Parents make about their Children

Recovery is Possible

When You Are Desperate for a Miracle

Decision-Making:
Explore a path to godly decision-making

This book and all other books from the same author are available at Christian bookstores and distributors worldwide.

They can also be obtained through online retail partners such as Amazon or by contacting the author at the address below:

Pastor Fatai Kasali
21-23 Stokescroft
Bristol
BS1 3PY
UK

Telephone:
00447727159581
E-mail: info@fkasali.com
Website: www.fkasali.com

www.ingramcontent.com/pod-product-compliance
Lightning Source LLC
Chambersburg PA
CBHW070119080526
44586CB00013B/1336